THE ROMAUNT OF THE ROSE

ILLUSTRATIONS

AS BYRDE IN BOUR	*Frontispiece*
IOLYF AND GAY	*To face page* 2
IN AT THE WIKET WENT I THO	8
THE DAUNCE	10
MYNSTRALES	12
THE GOD OF LOVE	14
YDELNESSE	16
LOVE PURSUING	20
THE BOTHOUN	22
THE THREE ARROWS OF LOVE	24
PEYNE	42
THE LOVER LISTENING TO REASOUN	44
UNTO MY FREEND, AND TOLDE HYM ALL	46
"A, BIALACOIL, MYN OWNE DEERE"	58
SWEET REASON	62
YOUTHE AND DELITE	66
"MI MODIR IS OF GRET PROWESSE"	78
"IF THAT I WERE GOD OF RICHESSE"	80
DAME ABSTINENCE-STREYNED	84
THE END	102

Of the above Illustrations, the Frontispiece and those facing pages 2, 10, 16, 20, 42, 44, 46, 80, and 102 are by KEITH HENDERSON; those facing pages 8, 12, 14, 22, 24, 58, 62, 66, 78, and 84 are by NORMAN WILKINSON.

HERE BEGINS THE ROMAUNT OF THE ROSE BY GUILLAUME DE LORRIS AND JEHAN DE MEUNG: RENDERED OUT OF THE FRENCH INTO ENGLISH BY GEOFFREY CHAUCER

MANY men sayn that in sweveninges
Ther nys but fables and lesynges;
But men may some swevenes sene
Whiche hardely that false ne bene,
But afterwarde ben apparaunt.
This maye I drawe to warraunt
An authour that hight Macrobes,
That halte nat dremes false ne lees,
But undothe us the avysioun
That whilom mette kyng Cipioun.
And who-so saith, or weneth it be
A jape, or elles nycete,
To wene that dremes after falle,
Lette who so lyste a fole me calle.
For this trowe I, and say for me,
That dremes signifiaunce be
Of good and harme to many wightes,
That dremen in her slepe a nyghtes
Ful many thynges covertly,
That fallen after al openly.

Within my twenty yere of age,
Whan that Love taketh his cariage
Of yonge folke, I wente soone
To bedde, as I was wont to done,
And faste I slepte; and in slepyng
Me mette suche a swevenyng
That lyked me wonder wele.
But in that sweven is never a dele
That it nys afterwarde befalle,
Ryght as this dreme wol tel us alle.

Nowe this dreme wol I ryme a-right
To make your hertes gaye and lyght,
For Love it prayeth and also
Commaundeth me that it be so.
And if there any aske me,
Whether that it be he or she,
Howe [wil I] this booke whiche is here
Shal hatte, that I rede you here;
It is the Romance of the Rose,
In whiche al the Arte of Love I close.

The mater fayre is of to make:
God graunt me in gree that she it take
For whom that it begonnen is!
And that is she that hath y-wis
So mochel pris, and therto she
So worthy is biloved to be
That she wel ought of pris and ryght
Be cleped Rose of every wight.

That it was May me thoughte tho—
It is .V. yere or more ago—
That it was May thus dremed me,
In tyme of love and jolite,
That al thing gynneth waxen gay.
For ther is neither busk nor hay
In May that it nyl shrouded bene,
And it with newe leves wrene.
These wodes eek recoveren grene
That drie in wynter ben to sene.
And the erthe wexith proude withalle
For swote dewes that on it falle,
And [al] the pore estat forgette
In which that wynter had it sette.
And than bycometh the ground so proude,
That it wole have a newe shroude,
And makith so queynt his robe and faire
That it hath hewes an hundred payre,

Of gras and flouris, ynde and pers,
And many hewes ful dyvers.
That is the robe I mene, y-wis,
Through whiche the ground to preisen is.

The byrdes that han lefte her song
While thei suffride cold so strong,
In wedres gryl and derk to sight,
Ben in May, for the sonne bright,
So glade that they shewe in syngyng,
That in her hertis is sich lykyng,
That they mote syngen and be light.
Than doth the nyghtyngale hir myght
To make noyse and syngen blythe;
Than is blisful many sithe
The chelaundre and [the] papyngay.
Than yonge folk entenden ay
Forto ben gay and amorous.
The tyme is than so saverous,
Hard is the hert that loveth nought
In May, whan al this mirth is wrought;
Whan he may on these braunches here
The smale briddes syngen clere
Her blesful swete song pitous.
And in this sesoun delytous,
Whan love affraieth alle thing,
Me thoughte a-nyght, in my sleping
Right in my bed, ful redily
That it was by the morowe erly,
And up I roos, and gan me clothe.
Anoon I wisshe myn hondis bothe.
A sylvre nedle forth y droughe
Out of an aguler queynt ynoughe,
And gan this nedle threde anon;
For out of toun me list to gon
The song of briddes forto here,
That in thise buskes syngen clere.
And in the swete seson that lefe is,
With a threde bastyng my slevis,
Alone I wente in my plaiyng,
The smale foules song harknyng,
That peyned hem ful many peyre
To synge on bowes blosmed feyre.
Iolyf and gay, ful of gladnesse,
Toward a ryver gan I me dresse,
That I herd renne faste by,
For fairer plaiyng non saugh I
Than playen me by that ryvere.
For from an hill that stood ther nere,
Cam doun the streme ful stif and bold;
Cleer was the water and as cold
As any welle is, soth to seyne.
And somdele lasse it was than Seyne,
But it was strayghter, wel away;
And never saugh I, er that day,
The watir that so wel lyked me,
And wondir glad was I to se
That lusty place and that ryvere.
And with that watir that ran so clere
My face I wysshe. Tho saugh I well
The botme paved everydell
With gravel ful of stones shene.
The medewe softe, swote, and grene,
Beet right on the watir syde.
Ful clere was than the morowtyde,
And ful attempre, out of drede.
Tho gan I walke thorough the mede,
Dounward ay in my pleiyng
The ryver syde costeiyng.
And whan I had a while goon,
I saugh a gardyn right anoon,
Ful long and brood, and euerydell
Enclosed was, and walled well
With highe walles enbatailled,
Portraied without and wel entailled
With many riche portraitures.
And bothe the ymages and peyntures
Gan I biholde bysyly;

IOLYF AND GAY

Of gras and flouris, ynde and pers,
And many hewes ful dyvers.
That is the robe I mene, y-wis,
Through whiche the ground to preisen is.

The byrdes that han lefte her song
While thei suffride cold so strong,
In wedres gryl and derk to sight,
Ben in May, for the sonne bright,
So glade that they shewe in syngyng,
That in her hertis is sich lykyng,
That they mote syngen and be light.
Than doth the nyghtyngale hir myght
To make noyse and syngen blythe;
Than is blisful many sithe
The chelaundre and [the] papyngay.
Than yonge folk entenden ay
Forto ben gay and amorous.
The tyme is than so saverous,
Hard is the hert that loveth nought
In May, whan al this mirth is wrought;
Whan he may on these braunches here
The smale briddes syngen clere
Her blesful swete song pitous.
And in this sesoun delytous,
Whan love affirmeth alle thing,
Me thoughte a-nyght, in my sleping
Right in my bed, ful redily
That it was by the morowe erly,
And up I roos, and gan me clothe.
Anoon I wisshe myn hondis bothe.
A sylvre nedle forth y droughe
Out of an aguler queynt ynoughe,
And gan this nedle threde anon.
For out of toun me list to gon
The song of briddes forto here,
That in thise buskes syngen clere.
And in the swete seson that lefe is,
With a threde bastyng my slevis
Alone I wente in my playyng,
The smale foules song harknyng,
That peyned hem ful many peyre
To synge on bowes blosmed feyre.
Iolyf and gay, ful of gladnesse,
Toward a ryver gan I me dresse,
That I herd renne faste by,
For fairer playyng non saugh I
Than playen me by that ryvere.
For from an hill that stood ther nere,
Cam doun the streme ful stif and bold;
Cleer was the water and as cold
As any welle is, soth to seyne.
And somdele lasse it was than Seyne,
But it was strayghter, wel away,
And never saugh I, er that day,
The watir that so wel lyked me,
And wondir glad was I to se
That lusty place and that ryvere.
And with that watir that ran so clere
My face I wysshe. Tho saugh I well
The botme paved everydell
With gravel ful of stones shene.
The medewe softe, swote, and grene,
Beet right on the watir syde.
Ful clere was than the morowtyde,
And ful attempre, out of drede
Tho gan I walke through the mede,
Dounward ay in my pleiyng
The ryver syde costeiyng.
And whan I had a while goon,
I saugh a gardyn right anoon,
Ful long and brood, and everydell
Enclosed was, and walled well
With highe walles enbatailled,
Portraied without and wel entailled
With many riche portraitures
And bothe the ymages and peyntures
Gan I biholde bisyly.

And I wole telle you redyly
Of thilk ymages the semblaunce,
As fer as I have remembraunce.

Amydde saugh I Hate stonde,
That for hir wrathe, yre, and onde
Semede to ben a meveresse,
An angry wight, a chideresse;
And ful of gyle and felle corage
By semblaunt was that ilk ymage.
And she was no thyng wel arraied,
But lyk a wode womman afraied.
Y-frounced foule was hir visage
And grennyng for dispitous rage;
Hir nose snorted up for tene.
Ful hidous was she forto sene,
Ful foule and rusty was she this;
Her heed y-writhen was, y-wis,
Ful grymly with a greet towayle.

An ymage of another entayle
A lyft half was hir faste by;
Hir name above hir heed saugh I,
And she was called Felonye.
Another ymage, that Vilanye
Y-clepid was, saugh I and fonde
Upon the wal on hir right honde.
Vilany was lyk somdel
That other ymage, and, trustith wel,
She semede a wikked creature.
By countenaunce in portrayture
She semed be ful dispitous,
And eek ful proude and outragious.
Wel coude he peynte, I undirtake,
That sich ymage coude make.
Ful foule and cherlysshe semed she,
And eek vylayneus forto be,
And litel coude of norriture
To worshipe any creature.

And next was peynted Coveitise,
That eggith folk in many gise
To take and yeve right nought ageyne,
And gret tresouris up to leyne.
And that is she that for usure
Leneth to many a creature,
The lasse for the more wynnyng,
So coveteise is her brennyng.
And that is she for penyes fele,
That techith forto robbe and stele
These theves and these smale harlotes;
And that is routh, for by her throtes
Ful many oon hangith at the laste.
She makith folk compasse and caste
To taken other folkis thyng
Through robberie or myscounting.
And that is she that makith trechoures
And she makith false pleadoures,
That, with hir termes and hir domes,
Doon maydens, children, & eek gromes
Her heritage to forgo.
Ful croked were hir hondis two,
For coveitise is evere wode
To gripen other folkis gode;
Coveityse for hir wynnyng
Ful leef hath other mennes thing.

Another ymage set saugh I
Next Coveitise faste by,
And she was clepid Avarice.
Ful foule in peyntyng was that vice,
Ful fade and caytif was she eek,
And also grene as ony leek.
So yvel hewed was hir colour
Hir semed to have lyved in langour;
She was lyk thyng for hungre deed,
That ladde hir lyf oonly by breed
Kneden with eisel strong and egre;
And therto she was lene and megre.

And she was clad ful porely
Al in an old torn courtepy,
As she were al with doggis torne;
And both bihynde and eke biforne
Clouted was she beggarly.
A mantyl henge hir faste by,
Upon a perche weike and small,
A burnet cote henge therwith-all,
Furred with no menyvere
But with a furre rough of here,
Of lambe skynnes hevy and blake,
It was ful old I undirtake,
For Avarice to clothe hir well
Ne hastith hir neveradell.
For certeynly it were hir loth
To weren ofte that ilke cloth;
And if it were forwered she
Wolde have ful gret necessite
Of clothyng, er she bought hir newe,
Al were it bad of woll and hewe.
This Avarice hilde in hir hande
A purs that henge [doun] by a bande,
And that she hidde and bonde so strong,
Men must abyde wondir long,
Out of that purs er ther come ought;
For that ne cometh not in hir thought.
It was not, certein, hir entent
That fro that purs a peny went.

And by that ymage nygh ynough
Was peynted ENVYE, that never lough,
Nor never wel in hir herte ferde,
But if she outher saugh or herde
Som gret myschaunce, or gret disese.
No thyng may so moch hir plese
As myschef and mysaventure;
Or whan she seeth discomfiture
Upon ony worthy man falle,
That likith hir wel with alle.
She is ful glade in hir corage,
If she se any grete lynage
Be brought to nought in shamful wise.
And if a man in honour rise,
Or by his witte or by his prowesse,
Of that hath she gret hevynesse.
For trustith wel she goth nygh wode,
Whan any chaunge happith gode.
Envie is of such crueltee
That feith ne trouth[e] holdith she
To freend ne felawe, bad or good
Ne she hath kynne noon of hir blood,
That she nys ful her enemye;
She nolde, I dar seyn hardelye,
Hir owne fadir ferde well.
And sore abieth she everydell
Hir malice and hir male talent,
For she is in so gret turment
And hath such [wo] whan folk doth good.
That nygh she meltith for pure wood;
Hir herte kervyth and so brekith,
That god the puple wel a-wrekith.
Envie, i-wis, shal nevere lette
Som blame upon the folk to sette;
I trowe that if Envie, i-wis,
Knewe the beste man that is
On this side, or biyonde the see,
Yit somewhat lakken hym wolde she;
And if he were so hende and wis,
That she ne myght al abate his pris,
Yit wolde she blame his worthynesse,
Or by hir wordis make it lesse.
I saugh Envie in that peyntyng
Hadde a wondirful lokyng,
For she ne lokide but awrie,
Or overthart all baggyngly.
And she hadde a foule usage,
She myght loke in no visage
Of man or womman forth-right pleyn,

But shette hir one eye for disdeyn;
So for Envie brenned she,
Whan she myght any man y-se
That faire or worthi were, or wise,
Or elles stode in folkis pryse.

Sorwe was peynted next Envie
Upon that wall of masonrye,
But wel was seyn in hir colour
That she hadde lyved in langour;
Hir semede to have the jaunyce.
Nought half so pale was Avarice,
Nor no thyng lyk [as] of lenesse;
For sorowe, thought, and gret distresse,
That she hadde suffred day and nyght,
Made hir ful yolwe and no thyng bright,
Ful fade, pale, and megre also.
Was never wight yit half so wo
As that hir semede forto be,
Nor so fulfilled of ire as she.
I trowe that no wight myght hir please,
Nor do that thyng that myght hir ease;
Nor she ne wolde hir sorowe slake
Nor comfort noon unto hir take,
So depe was hir wo bigonnen
And eek hir hert in angre ronnen.
A sorowful thyng wel semed she,
Nor she hadde no thyng slowe be
Forto forcracchen al hir face,
And forto rent in many place
Hir clothis, and forto tere hir swire,
As she that was fulfilled of ire.
And al to-torn lay eek hir here
Aboute hir shuldris here and there,
As she that hadde it al to-rent
For angre, and for maltalent.
And eek I telle you certeynly
How that she wepe ful tendirly.
In worlde nys wyght so harde of herte
That had [he] sene her sorowes smerte,
That nolde have had of her pyte,
So wo begone a thyng was she.
She al to-dassht her-selfe for woo,
And smote togyder her hondes two.
To sorowe was she ful ententyfe
That woful rechelesse caytyfe;
Her roughte lytel of playing
Or of clypping, or [of] kissyng;
For who so sorouful is in herte,
Him luste not to play ne sterte,
Ne for to dauncen, ne to synge,
Ne may his herte in temper bringe,
To make joye on even or morowe,
For joy is contrarie unto sorowe.

Elde was paynted after this,
That shorter was a foote, i-wys,
Than she was wonte in her yonghede.
Unneth her selfe she mighte fede;
So feble and eke so olde was she
That faded was al her beaute.
Ful salowe was waxen her colour;
Her heed for hore was whyte as flour,
I-wys great qualme ne were it none,
Ne synne, al though her lyfe were gone,
Al woxen was her body unwelde,
And drie and dwyned al for elde.
A foule forwelked thyng was she,
That whylom rounde and softe had be;
Her eeres shoken faste withall,
As from her heed they wolde fall;
Her face frounced and forpyned,
And bothe her hondes lorne, fordwyned.
So olde she was that she ne went
A foote, but it were by potent.
The tyme that passeth nyght and daye,
And restelesse travayleth aye,
And steleth from us so prively,

That to us semeth so sykerly
That it in one poynt dwelleth ever;
And certes it ne resteth never,
But gothe so faste, and passeth aye,
That there nys man that thynke may
What tyme that nowe present is;
Asketh at these clerkes this.
For [or] men thynke it redily
Thre tymes ben y-passed by.
The tyme that may not sojourne,
But goth and may never retourne,
As watir that doun renneth ay,
But never drope retourne may.
Ther may no thing as tyme endure,
Metall nor erthely creature;
For alle thing it frette and shall.
The tyme eke that chaungith all,
And all doth waxe and fostred be,
And alle thing distroieth he;
The tyme that eldith our auncessours,
And eldith kynges and emperours,
And that us alle shal overcomen
Er that deth us shal have nomen;
The tyme, that hath al in welde
To elden folk, had maad hir elde
So ynly, that to my witing,
She myght[e] helpe hir silf no thing,
But turned ageyn unto childhede.
She had no thing hir silf to lede,
Ne witte ne pithe in hir holde
More than a child of two yeer olde.
But natheles I trowe that she
Was faire sumtyme, and fresh to se,
Whan she was in hir rightful age;
But she was past al that passage,
And was a doted thing bicomen.
A furred cope on had she nomen,
Wel had she clad hir silf and warme,
For colde myght elles don hir harme.
These olde folk have alwey colde,
Her kynde is sich whan they ben olde.

Another thing was don there write,
That semede lyk an ipocrite,
And it was clepid Poope Holy.
That ilk is she that pryvely
Ne spareth never a wikked dede
Whan men of hir taken noon hede
And maketh hir outward precious
With pale visage and pitous,
And semeth a simple creature.
But ther nys no mysaventure
That she ne thenkith in hir corage.
Ful lyk to hir was that ymage,
That makid was lyk hir semblaunce.
She was ful symple of countenaunce
And she was clothed and eke shod
As she were, for the love of god,
Yolden to relygioun,
Sich semede hir devocioun.
A sauter helde she faste in honde,
And bisily she gan to fonde
To make many a feynt praiere
To god, and to his seyntis dere.
Ne she was gay, ne fresh, ne jolyf,
But semede to be ful ententyf
To gode werkis and to faire,
And therto she had on an haire;
Ne certis she was fatt no thing,
But semed wery for fasting;
Of colour pale and deed was she.
From hir the gate ay werned be
Of Paradys, that blisful place.
For sich folk maketh lene her face,
As Crist seith in his Evangile,
To gete prys in toun a while;
And for a litel glorie veigne
They lesen god and ek his reigne.

nd alderlast of everychon
/as peynted POVERT al aloon,
hat not a peny hadde in holde,
ll though she hir clothis solde,
nd though she shulde an honged be;
or nakid as a worme was she,
nd if the wedir stormy were,
or colde she shulde have dyed there.
he nadde on but a streit olde sak,
nd many a cloute on it ther stak;
his was hir cote and hir mantell,
o more was there, never a dell,
o clothe hir with, I undirtake;
rete leyser hadde she to quake.
nd she was putt, that I of talke, corner/
er fro these other, up in an halke; hiding place
here lurked and there coured she.
or pover thing, where so it be,
shamefast and dispised ay;
cursed may wel be that day
hat povere man conceyved is,
or god wote al to selde, i-wys,
ony povere man wel fedde
r wel araied or [wel] cledde,
r welbiloved in sich wise
n honour that he may arise.
lle these thingis well avised,
s I have you er this devysed,
Vith gold and asure over all
epeynted were upon the wall.
quare was the wall and high sumdell.
nclosed and barred well,
n stede of hegge, was that gardyne;
ome nevere shepherde therynne.
nto that gardyn wel y-wrought
Vho so that me coude have brought
y laddre, or elles by degre,
t wolde wel have liked me,
or sich solace, sich joie and play
I trowe that nevere man ne say,
As was in that place delytous.
The gardeyn was not daungerous
To herberwe briddes many oon,
So riche a yerde was nevere noon
Of briddes songe and braunches grene;
Therynne were briddes mo I wene
Than ben in all the rewme of Fraunce.
Ful blisful was the accordaunce
Of swete and pitous songe thei made;
For all this world it owghte glade.
And I my-silf so mery ferde,
Whan I her blisful songes herde,
That for an hundreth pounde nolde I,
If that the passage opunly
Hadde be unto me free,
That I nolde entren forto se
Thassemble—god kepe it fro care—
Of briddis whiche therynne ware.
That songen thorugh her mery throtes
Dauncis of love and mery notes.
Whan I thus herde foules synge,
I felle fast in a weymentyng,
By which art, or by what engyne,
I myght come into that gardyne.
But way I couthe fynde noon
Into that gardyne for to goon.
Ne nought wist I if that ther were
Eyther hole or place where,
By which I myght have entre.
Ne ther was noon to teche me,
For I was al aloone i-wys,
For-wo and angwishis of this.
Til atte last bithought I me,
That by no weye ne myght it be
That ther nas laddre, or wey to passe,
Or hole, into so faire a place.
Tho gan I go a full grete pas,
Envyronyng evene in compas

The closing of the square wall,
Tyl that I fonde a wiket small,
So shett that I ne myght in gon,
And other entre was ther noon.
Uppon this dore I gan to smyte
That was [so] fetys and so lite,
For other weye coude I not seke.
Ful long I shof, and knokkide eke,
And stood ful long and oft herknyng,
If that I herde ony wight comyng,
Til that dore of thilk entre
A mayden curteys openyde me.
Hir heer was as yelowe of hewe
As ony basyn scoured newe,
Hir flesh [as] tendre as is a chike,
With bente browis smothe and slyke;
And by mesure large were
The openyng of hir yen clere;
Hir nose of good proporcioun,
Hir yen grey as is a faucoun;
With swete breth and wel savoured,
Hir face white and wel coloured,
With litel mouth and rounde to see;
A clove chynne eke hadde she,
Hir nekke was of good fasoun,
In lengthe and gretnesse by resoun,
Withoute bleyne, scabbe, or royne;
Fro Iersalem unto Burgoyne
Ther nys a fairer nekke, i-wys,
To fele how smothe and softe it is.
Hir throte also white of hewe
As snowe on braunche snowed newe.
Of body ful wel wrought was she,
Men neded not in no cuntre
A fairer body forto seke.
And of fyn orfrays hadde she eke
A chapelet so semly oon
Ne werede never mayde upon.
And faire above that chapelet
A rose gerland had she sett.
She hadde [in honde] a gay mirrour,
And with a riche gold tresour
Hir heed was tressed, queyntely.
Hir sleves sewid fetously,
And forto kepe hir hondis faire
Of gloves white she had a paire.
And she hadde on a cote of grene
Of cloth of Gaunt, withouten wene.
Wel semyde by hir apparayle
She was not wont to gret travayle;
For whan she kempte was fetisly,
And wel arayed and richely,
Thanne had she don al hir journe.
For merye and wel bigoon was she,
She ladde a lusty lyf in May;
She hadde no thought by nyght ne day
Of no thyng, but it were oonly
To graythe hir wel and uncouthly.
Whan that this dore hadde opened me
This may[de] semely forto see,
I thanked hir as I best myght,
And axide hir how that she hight,
And what she was I axide eke.
And she to me was nought unmeke,
Ne of hir answer daungerous,
But faire answeride, and seide thus :—
" Lo, sir, my name is Ydelnesse;
So clepe men me, more and lesse;
Ful myghty and ful riche am I,
And that of oon thyng namely,
For I entende to no thyng,
But to my joye, and my pleyyng,
And forto kembe and tresse me.
Aqueynted am I and pryve
With Myrthe, lord of this gardyne,
That fro the lande Alexandryne
Made the trees hidre be fette
That in this gardyne ben y-sette.

IN AT THE WICKET WENT I THO

IN AT THE WICKET WENT I THO

propercioun,
s a faucoun;
and wel savoured,
nd wel coloured,
and rounde to see;
ke hadde she,
good fasoun,
etnesse by resoun,
wbbe, or royne;
o Burgoyne
nekke, I-wys,
the and softe it is.
hite of hewe
unche snw wel newe.
wrought was she,
n no cuntre
to seke.
s hadde she eke
ly oon
myde upon.
[illegible]

To graythe hir wel and uncouthly.
Whan that this dore hadde opened m[e]
This may[de] semely forto see,
I thanked hir as I best myght,
And axide hir how that she hight,
And what she was I axide eke.
And she to me was nought unmeke,
Ne of hir answer daungerous,
But faire answerde, and seide thus:—
"Lo, sir, my name is YDELNESSE;
So clepe men me, more and lesse;
Ful myghty and ful riche am I,
And that of oon thyng namely,
For I entende to no thyng,
But to my joye, and my pleyyng,
And forto kembe and tresse me.
Aqueynted am I and pryve
With Myrthe, lord of this gardyne,
That fro the lande Alexandryne
Made the trees hidre be sette
That in this gardyne ben y-sette.

And whan the trees were woxen on hight,
This wall, that stant heere in thi sight,
Dide Myrthe enclosen al aboute.
And these ymages al withoute
He dide hem bothe entaile and peynte,
That neithir ben jolyf ne queynte,
But they ben ful of sorowe and woo,
As thou hast seen a while agoo.
And ofte tyme hym to solace
Sir Myrthe cometh into this place,
And eke with hym cometh his meynee,
That lyven in lust and jolite.
And now is Myrthe therynne to here
The briddis, how they syngen clere,
The mavys and the nyghtyngale,
And other joly briddis smale.
And thus he walketh to solace
Hym and his folk, for swetter place
To pleyen ynne he may not fynde,
Al though he sought oon in-tyl Ynde.
The alther-fairest folk to see
That in this world may founde be
Hath Mirthe with hym in his route,
That folowen hym always aboute."
Whan Ydelnesse had tolde al this,
And I hadde herkned wel y-wys,
Thanne seide I to dame Ydelnesse:
"Now also wisly god me blesse,
Sith Myrthe that is so faire and fre
Is in this yerde with his meyne,
Fro thilk assemble, if I may,
Shal no man werne me to-day,
That I this nyght ne mote it see.
For wel wene I there with hym be
A faire and joly companye,
Fulfilled of all curtesie."
And forth, withoute wordis mo,
In at the wiket went I tho,
That Ydelnesse hadde opened me,
Into that gardyne faire to see.
And whan I was inne i-wys,
Myn herte was ful glad of this.
For wel wende I ful sikerly
Have ben in Paradys erthly;
So faire it was that, trusteth wel,
It semede a place espirituel.
For certys, as at my devys,
Ther is no place in Paradys
So good inne forto dwelle or be,
As in that gardyne, thoughte me.
For there was many a bridde syngyng
Thorough-out the yerde al thringyng.
In many places were nyghtyngales,
Alpes, fynches, and wodewales,
That in her swete song deliten.
In thilke places as they habiten,
There myght[e] men see many flokkes
Of turtles and [of] laverokkes.
Chalaundres fele sawe I there,
That wery, nygh forsongen were.
And thrustles, terins, and mavys,
That songen forto wynne hem prys,
And eke to sormounte in hir songe
That othere briddes hem amonge.
By note made faire servyse
These briddes that I you devise;
They songe her songe as faire and wele
As angels don espirituel.
And, trusteth wel, than I hem herde,
Ful lustily and wel I ferde,
For never yitt sich melodye
Was herd of man that myghte dye.
Sich swete song was hem amonge,
That me thought it no briddis songe,
But it was wondir lyk to be
Song of mermaydens of the see,
That, for her syngyng is so clere,
Though we mermaydens clepe hem here

In English as is oure usaunce,
Men clepe hem sereyns in Fraunce.
Ententif weren forto synge
These briddis, that nought unkunnyng
Were of her craft and apprentys,
But of song sotil and wys.
And certis, whan I herde her songe,
And sawe the grene place amonge,
In herte I wexe so wondir gay,
That I was never erst er that day
So jolyf, nor so wel bigoo,
Ne merye in herte, as I was thoo.
And than wist I and sawe ful well,
That Ydelnesse me served well,
That me putte in sich jolite.
Hir freend wel ought I forto be
Sith she the dore of that gardyne
Hadde opened, and me leten inne.
From hennes forth how that I wroughte,
I shal you tellen as me thoughte.
First wherof Myrthe served there,
And eke what folk there with hym were,
Withoute fable I wole discryve;
And of that gardyne eke as blyve
I wole you tellen aftir this
The faire fasoun all y-wys,
That wel y-wrought was for the nones.
I may not telle you all at ones,
But as I may and can, I shall
By ordre tellen you it all.
Ful faire servise, and eke ful swete,
These briddis maden, as they sete;
Layes of love ful wel sownyng,
They songen in their jargonyng;
Summe high and summe eke lowe songe
Upon the braunches grene y-spronge.
The swetnesse of her melodye
Made al myn herte in reverye.
And whan that I hadde herde, I trowe,
These briddis syngyng on a rowe,
Than myght I not withholde me
That I ne wente inne forto see
Sir Myrthe; for my desiryng
Was hym to seen, over alle thyng;
His countenaunce and his manere,
That sighte was to me ful dere.
Tho wente I forth on my right honde
Doun by a lytel path I fonde,
Of mentes full and fenell grene.
And faste by, withoute wene,
Sir Myrthe I fonde, and right anoon
Unto sir Myrthe gan I goon,
There as he was, hym to solace.
And with hym in that lusty place
So faire folk and so fresh had he,
That whan I sawe I wondred me
Fro whennes siche folk myght come,
So faire they weren all and some,
For they were lyk, as to my sighte,
To angels that ben fethered brighte.

This folk, of which I telle you soo,
Upon a karole wenten thoo.
A lady karolede hem, that hyght
GLADNESSE, [the] blisfull and the light.
Wel coude she synge and lustyly;
Noon half so wel and semely,
Couthe make in song sich refreynynge.
It sat hir wondir wel to synge;
Hir voice ful clere was and ful swete,
She was nought rude ne unmete,
But couthe ynow of sich doyng
As longeth unto karolyng.
For she was wont in every place
To syngen first, folk to solace,
For syngyng moost she gaf hir to,
No craft had she so leef to do.
Tho myghtist thou karoles sene,

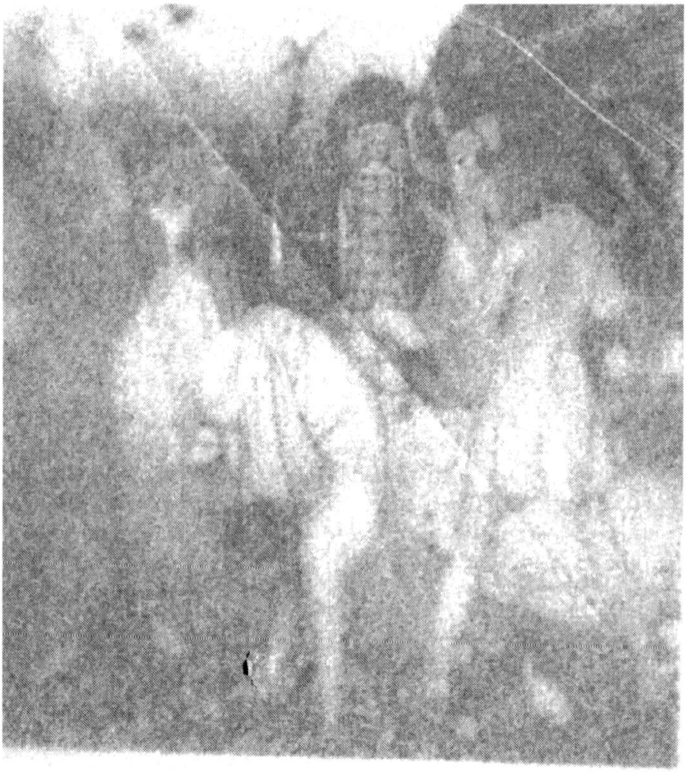

THE DAUNCE

And folk daunce and mery bene,
And make many a faire tournyng
Upon the grene gras springyng.
There myghtist thou see these flowtours,
Mynstrales, and eke jogelours,
That wel to synge dide her peyne;
Somme songe songes of Loreyne,
For in Loreyn her notes bee
Full swetter than in this contre.
There was many a tymbester,
And saillouris that I dar wel swere,
Couthe her craft ful parfitly;
The tymbres up ful sotilly,
They caste and hente full ofte,
Upon a fynger faire and softe,
That they [ne] failide never mo.
Ful fetys damyselles two,
Ryght yonge and full of semelyhede,
In kirtles and noon other wede
And faire tressed every tresse,
Hadde Myrthe doon, for his noblesse,
Amydde the karole forto daunce.
But herof lieth no remembraunce
How that they daunced queyntely;
That oon wolde come all pryvyly
Agayn that other, and whan they were
To-gidre almost, they threwe yfere
Her mouthis so that through her play
It semed as they kiste alway.
To dauncen well koude they the gise,
What shulde I more to you devyse;
Ne bode I never thennes go,
Whiles that I sawe hem daunce so.

Upon the karoll wonder faste
I gan biholde, til atte laste
A lady gan me forto espie;
And she was cleped Curtesie
The worshipfull, the debonaire,
I pray to god evere falle hir faire.
Ful curteisly she callede me,
"What do ye there, Beau ser?" quod she,
"Come [here], and if it lyke yow
To dauncen, dauncith with us now."
And I withoute tariyng
Wente into the karolyng.
I was abasshed never a dell,
But it to me liked right well
That Curtesie me cleped so,
And bad me on the daunce go.
For if I hadde durst, certeyn
I wolde have karoled right fayn,
As man that was to daunce blithe.
Thanne gan I loken ofte sithe
The shape, the bodies, and the cheres,
The countenaunce, and the maneres
Of all the folk that daunced there;
And I shal tell [you] what they were.

Ful faire was Myrthe, ful longe and high,
A fairer man I nevere sigh;
As rounde as appille was his face,
Ful rody and white in every place.
Fetys he was and wel beseye,
With metely mouth and yen greye,
His nose by mesure wrought ful right.
Crispe was his heer, and eek ful bright,
Hise shuldris of a large brede,
And smalish in the girdilstede.
He semed lyke a portreiture,
So noble he was of his stature,
So faire, so joly and so fetys,
With lymes wrought at poynt devys,
Delyver, smert, and of grete myght;
Ne sawe thou nevere man so lyght.
Of berde unnethe hadde he no thyng,
For it was in the firste spryng.
Ful yonge he was, and mery of thought;

And in samette with briddis wrought,
And with gold beten ful fetysly,
His body was clad ful richely.
Wrought was his robe in straunge gise
And al to-slytered for queyntise
In many a place lowe and hie;
And shode he was with grete maistrie,
With shoon decoped and with laas,
By druery and by solas,
His leef a rosyn chapelet
Hadde made and on his heed it set.

And wite ye who was his leef?
Dame Gladnesse there was hym so leef,
That syngith so wel with glad courage,
That from she was .XII. yeer of age,
She of hir love graunt hym made.
Sir Mirthe hir by the fynger hadde
Daunsyng, and she hym also;
Grete love was atwixe hem two.
Bothe were they faire and bright of
  hewe;
She semede lyke a rose newe
Of colour, and hir flesh so tendre
That with a brere smale and slendre
Men myght it cleve, I dar wel seyn;
Hir forheed frounceles, al pleyn;
Bent were hir [browne] browis two,
Hir yen greye and glad also,
That laugheden ay in hir semblaunt
First or the mouth, by covenaunt.
I not what of hir nose descryve,
So faire hath no womman alyve.
Hir heer was yelowe, and clere shynyng,
I wot no lady so likyng.
Of orfrays fresh was hir gerland;
I, which seyen have a thousand,
Saugh never y-wys no gerlond yitt,
So wel y-wrought of silk as it.
And in an overgilt samit
Cladde she was, by grete delit,
Of which hir leef a robe werede;
The myrier she in hir herte ferede.

And next hir wente, in hir other side,
The God of Love, that can devyde
Love, and as hym likith it be,
But he can cherles daunten, he,
And maken folkis pride fallen,
And he can wel these lordis thrallen,
And ladyes putt at lowe degre,
Whan he may hem to proude see.
This God of Love of his fasoun
Was lyke no knave, ne quystroun.
His beaute gretly was to preyse,
But of his robe to devise
I drede encombred forto be;
For nought y-clad in silk was he,
But all in floures and in flourettes,
I-paynted all with amorettes.
And with losenges, and scochouns,
With briddes, lybardes, and lyouns,
And other beestis wrought ful well,
His garnement was everydell
Y-portreied, and wrought with floures,
By dyvers medlyng of coloures.
Floures there were of many gise,
Y-sett by compas in assise;
Ther lakkide no flour to my dome,
Ne nought so mych as flour of brome,
Ne violete, ne eke pervynke,
Ne flour noon that man can on thynke;
And many a rose-leef ful longe,
Was entermelled ther amonge,
And also on his heed was sette
Of roses reed a chapelett.
But nyghtyngales, a full grete route
That flyen over his heed aboute,

MYNSTRALES

Was entermelled thee amonge,
That also on his heed was sette
Of roses reed a chapelet;
But nyghtyngales, a full grete route
That flyen over his heed aboute,

The leeves felden as they flyen;
And he was all with briddes wryen,
With popynjay, with nyghtyngale,
With chalaundre, and with wodewale,
With fynche, with lark, and with archaungell.
He semede as he were an aungell,
That doun were comen fro hevene clere.

Love hadd with hym a bachelere,
That he made alleweyes with hym be;
SWETE LOKYNG cleped was he.
This bachelere stode biholdyng
The daunce; and in his honde holdyng
Turke bowes two had he.
That oon of hem was of a tree
That bereth a fruyt of savour wykke,
Ful crokid was that foule stikke;
And knotty here and there also,
And blak as bery, or ony slo.
That other bowe was of a plante
Withouten wem, I dar warante,
Ful evene, and by proporcioun
Treitys and long, of good fasoun;
And it was peynted wel and thwyten,
And over al diapred and writen
With ladyes and with bachelerıs,
Full lyghtsom and glad of cheris.
These bowes two helde Swete-lokyng,
That semede lyk no gadelyng,
And ten brode arowis hılde he there,
Of which .V. in his righthond were;
But they were shaven well and dight,
Nokked and fethered aright,
And all they were with gold bygoon,
And strong‿poynted everychoon,
And sharpe forto kerven well.
But iren was ther noon, ne steell,
For al was golde, men myght it see,
Out-take the fetheres and the tree.
The swiftest of these arowis fyve
Out of a bowe forto dryve,
And beste fethered for to flee,
And fairest eke, was clepid Beaute;
That other arowe that hurteth lesse
Was clepid, as I trowe, Symplesse,
The thridde cleped was Fraunchise
That fethred was in noble wise,
With valour and with curtesye;
The fourthe was cleped Compaignye,
That hevy forto shoten ys;
But who so shetith right y-wys,
May therwith doon grete harme and wo.
The fifte of these, and laste also,
Faire-Semblaunt men that arowe calle,
The leeste grevous of hem alle,
Yit can it make a ful grete wounde.
But he may hope his soris sounde,
That hurt is with that arowe y-wys;
His wo the bette bistowed is,
For he may sonner have gladnesse;
His langour oughte be the lesse.
Five arowis were of other gise,
That ben ful foule to devyse,
For shaft and ende, soth forto telle,
Were also blak as fende in helle.
The first of hem is called Pride,
That‿other arowe next hym biside,
It was [y-]cleped Vylanye.
That arowe was al with felonye
Envenymed, and with spitous blame.
The thridde of hem was cleped Shame,
The fourthe Wanhope cleped is,
The fifte Newe-thought, y-wys.
These arowis that I speke of heere
Were alle fyve on oon maneere,
And alle were they resemblable.
To hem was wel sittyng and able,

The foule croked bowe hidous
That knotty was, and al roynous;
That bowe semede wel to shete
These arowis fyve, that ben unmete
And contrarye to that other fyve.
But though I telle not as blyve
Of her power, ne of her myght,
Herafter shal I tellen right
The soothe, and eke signyfiaunce;
As fer as I have remembraunce
All shal be seid, I undirtake,
Er of this book an ende I make

Now come I to my tale ageyn.
But aldirfirst I wole you seyn
The fasoun and the countenaunces
Of all the folk that on the daunce is.
The God of Love, jolyf and lyght,
Ladde on his honde a lady bright,
Of high prys and of grete degre;
This lady called was Beaute,
As an arowe of which I tolde,
Ful wel [y-]thewed was she holde;
Ne she was derk, ne broun, but bright,
And clere as [is] the mone lyght,
Ageyn whom all the sterres semen
But smale candels, as we demen.
Hir flesh was tendre as dewe of flour,
Hir chere was symple as byrde in bour,
As whyte as lylye or rose in rys;
Hir face gentyl and tretys,
Fetys she was, and smale to se;
No wyntred browis hadde she,
Ne popped hir, for it neded nought
To wyndre hir, or to peynte hir ought.
Hir tresses yelowe, and longe straughten,
Unto hir helys doun they raughten;
Hir nose, hir mouth, and eyhe, and cheke
Wel wrought, and all the remenaunt eke.
A ful grete savour and a swote
Me toucheth in myn herte rote,
As helpe me god, whan I remembre
Of the fasoun of every membre.
In world is noon so faire a wight;
For yonge she was, and hewed bright,
Sore plesaunt, and fetys with all,
Gente, and in hir myddill small.
Biside Beaute yede richesse,
An high lady of gret noblesse,
And gret of prys in every place;
But who so durste to hir trespace,
Or til hir folk, in word or dede,
He were full hardy, out of drede.
For bothe she helpe and hyndre may;
And that is nought of yisterday,
That riche folk have full gret myght
To helpe, and eke to greve a wyght.
The leste and grettest of valour
Diden Rychesse ful gret honour,
And besy weren hir to serve,
For that they wolde hir love deserve.
They cleped hir "Lady," grete and small;
This wide world hir dredith all,
This world is all in hir daungere.
Hir court hath many a losengere,
And many a traytour envyous,
That ben ful besy and curyous
Forto dispreisen and to blame
That best deserven love and name.
Bifore the folk, hem to bigilen,
These losengeris hem preyse, and smylen,
And thus the world with word anoynten;
And aftirward they prille, and poynten
The folk right to the bare boon,
Bihynde her bak whan they ben goon,
And foule abate the folkis prys.
Ful many a worthy man, y-wys
An hundrid, have do to dye

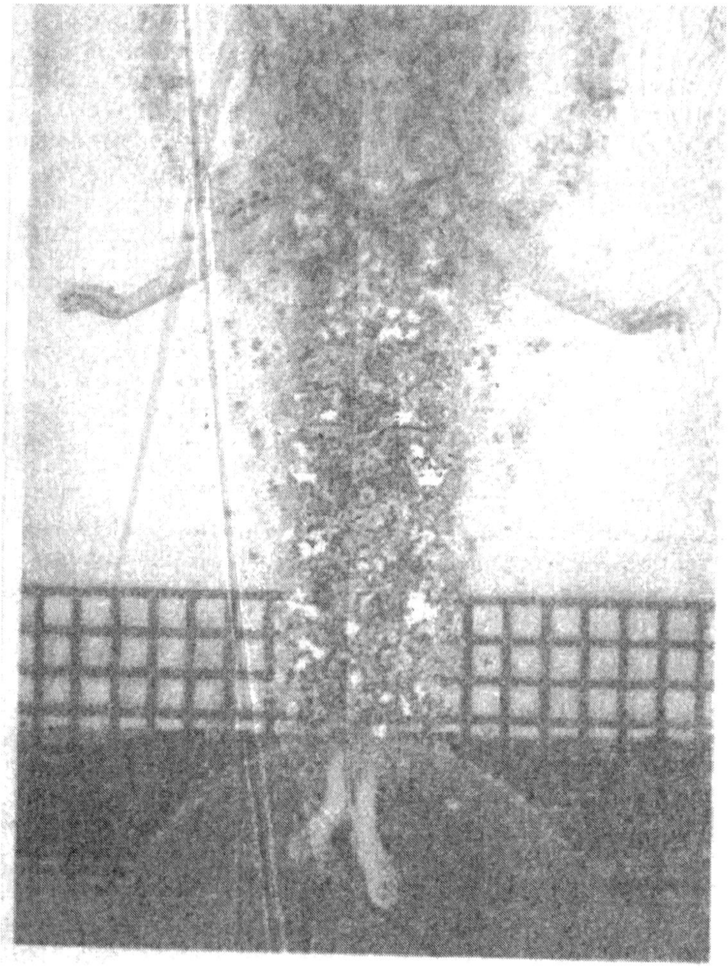

THE GOD OF LOVE

[illegible] xide
[illegible] rote,
[illegible] remembre
[illegible] membre.
[illegible] a wight;
[illegible] hewed bright,
[illegible] with all,
[illegible] small.
[illegible] richesse,
[illegible] noblesse,
And [illegible] every place;
But who so durste to hir trespace,
Or til hir folk, in word or dede,
He were full hardy, out of drede.
For bothe she helpe and hyndre may;
And that is nought of yisterday,
That riche folk have full gret myght
To helpe, and eke to greve a wyght.
The leste and grettest of valour
Diden Rychesse ful gret honour,
And besy weren hir to serve,
For that they wolde hir love deserve.
They cleped hir "Lady," grete and small;
This wide world hir dredith all,
This world is all in hir daungere.
Hir court hath many a losengere,
And many a traytour envyous,
That ben ful besy and curyous
Forto dispreisen and to blame
That best deserven love and name.
Bifore the folk, hem to bigilen,
These losengeris [illegible], and smylen;
And thus [illegible] anoynten;
And [illegible] and poynten
The folk [illegible] boon,
Bihynde [illegible] ben goon.
And [illegible] prys.
[illegible] wys
[illegible]

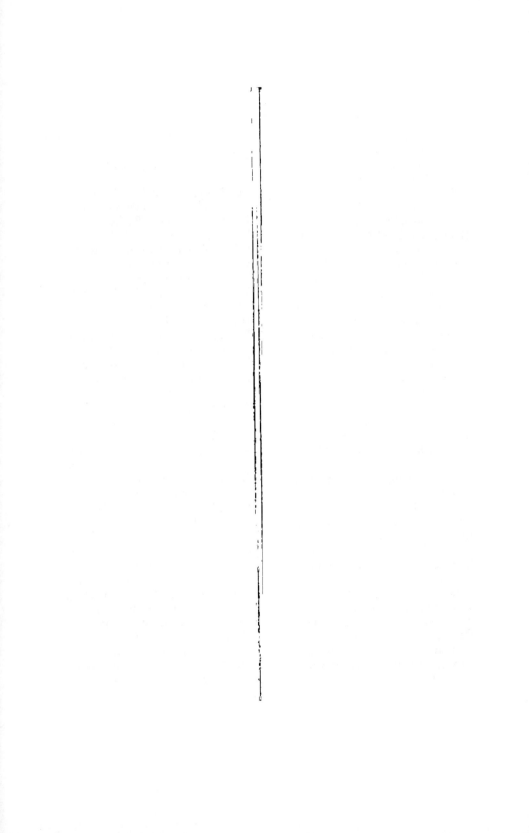

These losengers thorough flaterye;
And make folk ful straunge be
There hem oughte be pryve.
Wel yvel mote they thryve and thee,
And yvel arryved mote they be,
These losengers ful of envye;
No good man loveth her companye.
Richesse a robe of purpur on hadde,
Ne trowe not that I lye or madde,
For in this world is noon hir lyche,
Ne by a thousand deel so riche,
Ne noon so faire; for it ful well
With orfrays leyd was everydeell
And portraied in the ribanynges
Of dukes storyes, and of kynges,
And with a bend of gold tasseled,
And knoppis fyne of gold ameled.
Aboute hir nekke of gentyl entayle
Was shete the riche chevesaile,
In which ther was ful gret plente
Of stones clere and bright to see.
Rychesse a girdell hadde upon,
The bokele of it was of a stoon,
Of vertu gret and mochel of myght;
For who so bare the stoon so bright,
Of venym durst hym no thing doute,
While he the stoon hadde hym aboute.
That stoon was gretly forto love,
And, tyl a riche mannys byhove,
Worth all the gold in Rome and Frise.
The mourdaunt wrought in noble
 wise
Was of a stoon full precious,
That was so fyne and vertuous
That hole a man it koude make
Of palasie, and [of] tothe ake.
And yit the stoon hadde such a grace
That he was siker in every place,
All thilke day not blynde to bene,
That fastyng myght that stoon [have]
 seene.
The barres were of gold ful fyne
Upon a tyssu of satyne,
Full hevy, gret, and no thyng lyght,
In everiche was a besaunt-wight.
Upon the tresses of Richesse
Was sette a cercle, for noblesse,
Of brend gold that full lyghte shoon,
So faire trowe I was never noon.
But she were kunnyng for the nonys,
That koude devyse alle the stonys,
That in that cercle shewen clere.
It is a wondir thing to here,
For no man koude preyse or gesse
Of hem the valewe or richesse.
Rubyes there were, saphires, jagounces,
And emeraudes more than two ounces.
But all byfore ful sotilly
A fyn charboncle sette saugh I;
The stoon so clere was and so bright,
That also soone as it was nyght,
Men myght[e] seen to go for nede
A myle or two in lengthe and brede.
Sich lyght sprang oute of the stone,
That Richesse wondir brighte shone,
Bothe hir heed and all hir face,
And eke aboute hir al the place.

Dame Richesse on hir honde gan lede
A yong man full of semelyhede,
That she best loved of ony thing.
His lust was mych in housholding,
In clothyng was he ful fetys,
And loved to have well hors of prys;
He wende to have reproved be
Of theft or moordre, if that he
Hadde in his stable ony hakeney.
And therfore he desired ay

To be aqueynted with Richesse,
For all his purpos, as I gesse,
Was forto make gret dispense
Withoute wernyng or diffense;
And Richesse myght it wel sustene
And hir dispence well mayntene,
And hym alwey sich plente sende
Of gold and silver forto spende
Withoute lakking or daunger,
As it were poured in a garner.

And after on the daunce wente
LARGESSE, that sette al hir entente
Forto be honourable and free.
Of Alexandres kyn was she;
Hir moste joye was y-wys
Whan that she yaf, and seide, "Have this."
Not Avarice, the foule caytyf,
Was half to gripe so ententyf,
As Largesse is to yeve and spende;
And god ynough alwey hir sende,
So that the more she yaf awey
The more y-wys she hadde alwey.
Gret loos hath Largesse and gret pris,
For bothe wyse folk and unwys
Were hooly to hir baundon brought,
So wel with yiftes hath she wrought.
And if she hadde an enemy,
I trowe that she coude tristely
Make hym full soone hir freend to be,
So large of yift and free was she.
Therfore she stode in love and grace
Of riche and pover in every place.
A full gret fool is he y-wys
That bothe riche and nygart is;
A lord may have no maner vice
That greveth more than avarice;
For nygart never with strengthe of honde
May wynne gret lordship or londe;
For freendis all to fewe hath he
To doon his will perfourmed be.
And who so wole have freendis heere,
He may not holde his tresour deere.
For by ensample I telle this,
Right as an adamaund y-wys
Can drawen to hym sotylly
The yren that is leid therby,
So drawith folkes hertis y-wis
Silver and gold that yeven is.
Largesse hadde on a robe fresh
Of riche purpur Sarsynesh.
Wel fourmed was hir face and cleere,
And opened hadde she hir colere;
For she right there hadde in present
Unto a lady maad present
Of a gold broche, ful wel wrought.
And certys it myssatte hir nought,
For thorough hir smokke wrought with silk
The flesh was seen as white as mylk.
Largesse, that worthy was and wys,
Hilde by the honde a knyght of prys,
Was sibbe to Artour of Britaigne,
And that was he that bare the ensaigne
Of worship, and the gounfanoun.
And yit he is of sich renoun
That men of hym seye faire thynges
Byfore barouns, erles, and kynges.
This knyght was comen all newly
Fro [a] tourneiyng faste by.

Ther hadde he don gret chyvalrie
Through his vertu and his maistrie,
And for the love of his lemman
He caste doun many a doughty man.
And next hym daunced dame FRAUNCHISE
Arayed in full noble gyse.

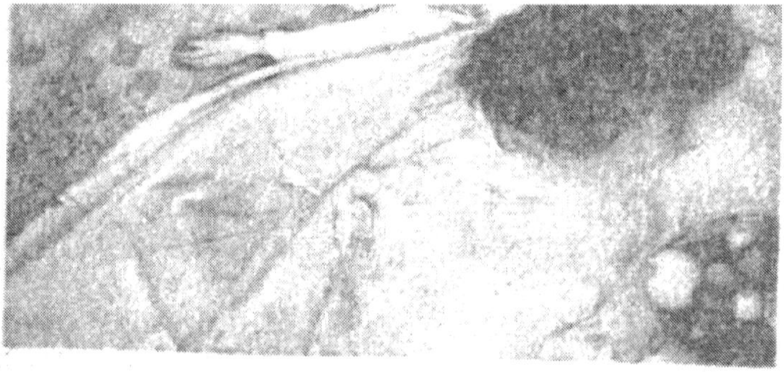

YDELNESSE

That men of hym seye faire thynges
Byfore barouns, erles, and kynges.
This knyght was comen all newly
Fro [a] tourneiyng faste by.

Ther hadde he don gret chyvalrie
Through his vertu and his maistrie,
And for the love of his lemman
He caste doun many a doughty man
And next hym daunced dame FRAUNC[illegible]
Arayed in full noble gyse.

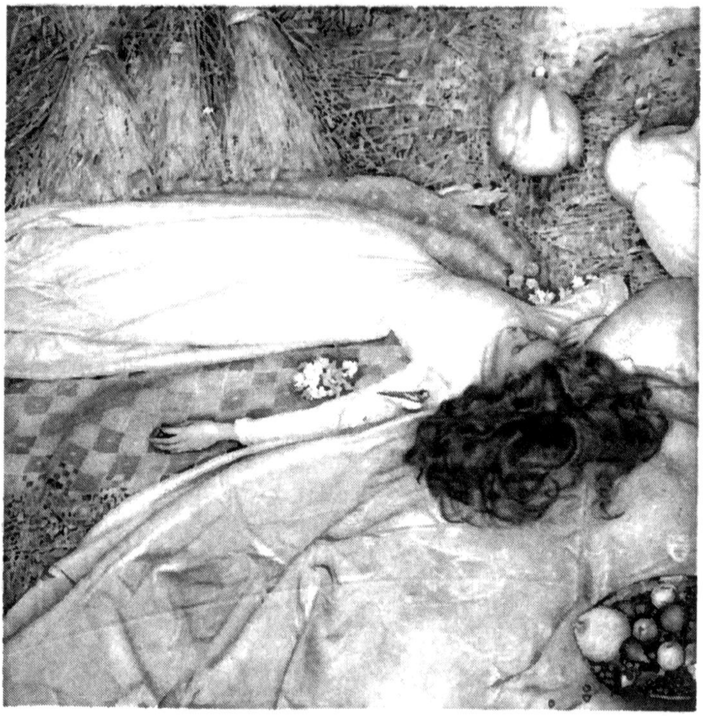

he was not broune ne dunne of hewe,
ut white as snowe y-fallen newe.
ir nose was wrought at poynt devys,
or it was gentyl and tretys,
Vith eyen gladde and browes bente,
ir here doun to hir helis wente;
nd she was symple as dowve on tree.
ul debonaire of herte was she;
he durst neither seyn ne do
ut that that hir longed to.
nd if a man were in distresse,
nd for hir love in hevynesse
ir herte wolde have full gret pite,
he was so amiable and free.
or were a man for hir bistadde,
he wolde ben right sore adradde
hat she dide over gret outrage;
ut she hym holpe his harme to aswage,
ir thought it ell a vylanye.
nd she hadde on a sukkenye
hat not of hempe ne heerdis was;
o fair was noon in all Arras.
ord, it was ridled fetysly!
her nas nat a poynt trewely
hat it nas in his right assise.
ull wel y-clothed was Fraunchise,
or ther is no cloth sittith bet
n damysell than doth roket;
womman wel more fetys is
n roket than in cote y-wis.
he whyte roket, rydled faire,
itokeneth that full debonaire
nd swete was she that it bere.

i hir daunced a bachelere;
can not telle you what he hight,
ut faire he was and of good hight,
ll hadde he be, I sey no more,
he lordis sone of Wyndesore.

And next that daunced Curtesye,
That preised was of lowe and hye,
For neither proude ne foole was she.
She forto daunce called me,
I pray god yeve hir right good grace,
Whanne I come first into the place,
She was not nyce ne outrageous,
But wys and ware and vertuous;
Of faire speche and of faire answere,
Was never wight mysseid of here,
Ne she bar rancour to no wight.
Clere broune she was and therto bright
Of face, of body avenaunt;
I wot no lady so plesaunt.
She were worthy forto bene
An emperesse or crowned quene.

And by hir wente a knyght dauncyng,
That worthy was and wel spekyng,
And ful wel koude he don honour.
The knyght was faire and styf in stour,
And in armure a semely man,
And welbiloved of his lemman.

Faire Idilnesse thanne saugh I,
That alwey was me faste by;
Of hir have I withoute fayle
Told yow the shap and apparayle.
For, as I seide, loo that was she
That dide to me so gret bounte,
That she the gate of the gardyn
Undide and lete me passen in.

And after daunced, as I gesse,
Youthe fulfilled of lustynesse,
That nas not yit XII yeer of age,
With herte wylde and thought volage.
Nyce she was, but she ne mente
Noon harme ne slight in hir entente,

But oonly lust and jolyte;
For yonge folk wele witen ye
Have lytel thought but on her play.
Hir lemman was biside alway
In sich a gise that he hir kyste
At alle tymes that hym lyste;
That all the daunce myght it see,
They make no force of pryvete;
For who spake of hem yvel or well,
They were ashamed neveradell,
But men myght seen hem kisse there,
As it two yonge dowves were.
For yong was thilke bachelere,
Of beaute wot I noon his pere,
And he was right of sich an age
As Youthe his leef, and sich corage.

The lusty folk that daunced there,
And also other that with hem were,
That weren all of her meyne,
Ful hende folk and wys and free
And folk of faire port trewely
They weren alle comunly.
Whanne I hadde seen the countenaunces
Of hem that ladden thus these daunces,
Thanne hadde I will to gon and see
The gardyne that so lyked me,
And loken on these faire loreres,
On pyntrees, cedres, and olmeris.
The daunces thanne y-ended were,
For many of hem that daunced there
Were with her loves went awey,
Undir the trees to have her pley.
A lord, they lyved lustyly!
A gret fool were he sikirly
That nolde his thankes such lyf lede.
For this dar I seyn oute of drede,
That who so myghte so wel fare,
For better lyf durst hym not care;
For ther nys so good paradys
As to have a love at his devys.
Oute of that place wente I thoo,
And in that gardyn gan I goo,
Pleyyng alonge full meryly.
The God of Love full hastely
Unto hym Swete-Lokyng clepte.
No lenger wolde he that he kepte
His bowe of gold, that shoon so bright;
He bad hym bend it anoon ryght.
And he full soone sette an-ende,
And at a braid he gan it bende;
And toke hym of his arowes fyve,
Full sharp and redy forto dryve.

Now god that sittith in mageste,
Fro deedly woundes he kepe me,
If so be that he hadde me shette!
For if I with his arowe mette,
It hadde me greved sore y-wys.
But I, that no thyng wist of this,
Wente up and doun full many awey,
And he me folwed faste alwey;
But no where wolde I reste me,
Till I hadde in all the gardyn be.

The gardyn was by mesuryng
Right evene and square; in compassing
It was as long as it was large.
Of fruyt hadde every tree his charge,
But it were any hidous tree,
Of which ther were two or three.
There were, and that wote I full well,
Of pome garnettys a full gret dell,
That is a fruyt full well to lyke,
Namely to folk whanne they ben sike.
And trees there were of gret foisoun
That baren nottes in her sesoun
Such as men note mygges calle,

That swote of savour ben withalle;
And almanderes gret plente,
Fyges, and many a date tree,
There wexen, if men hadde nede,
Thorough the gardyn in length and brede.
Ther was eke wexyng many a spice,
As clowe-gelofre, and lycorice,
Gyngevre, and greyn de Paradys,
Canell, and setewale of prys,
And many a spice delitable
To eten whan men rise fro table.
And many homly trees ther were
That peches, coynes, and apples beere,
Medlers, plowmes, perys, chesteynis,
Cherys, of which many oon fayne is,
Notes, aleys, and bolas,
That forto seen it was solas;
With many high lorer and pyn
Was renged clene all that gardyn,
With cipres and with olyveris,
Of which that nygh no plente heere is.
There were elmes grete and stronge,
Maples, asshe, oke, aspe, planes longe,
Fyne ew, popler, and lyndes faire,
And othere trees full many a payre—
What shulde I tel you more of it?
There were so many trees yit,
That I shulde al encombred be
Er I had rekened every tree.

These trees were sette, that I devyse,
One from another in assyse
Fyve fadome or sixe, I trowe so;
But they were hye and great also,
And for to kepe out wel the sonne,
The croppes were so thicke y-ronne,
And every braunche in other knette,
And ful of grene leves sette,
That sonne myght there none discende,
Lest [it] the tender grasses shende.
There myght men does and roes y-se,
And of squyrels ful great plente
From bowe to bowe alwaye lepynge;
Connes there were also plaiynge,
That comyn out of her clapers,
Of sondrie colours and maners,
And maden many a tourneiyng
Upon the fresshe grasse spryngyng.

In places sawe I welles there
In whiche there no frogges were,
And fayre in shadowe was every welle.
But I ne can the nombre telle
Of stremys smal, that by devyse
Myrthe had done come through condyse;
Of whiche the water in rennyng
Gan make a noyse ful lykyng.

About the brinkes of these welles
And by the stremes over al elles
Sprange up the grasse, as thicke y-set
And softe as any veluet,
On whiche men myght his lemman ley
As on a fetherbed to pley,
For the erthe was ful softe and swete.
Through moisture of the welle wete
Spronge up the sote grene gras
As fayre, as thicke, as myster was.
But moche amended it the place
That therthe was of suche a grace
That it of floures hath plente,
That bothe in somer and wynter be.
There sprange the vyolet al newe,
And fresshe pervynke riche of hewe,
And floures yelowe, white, and rede,
Suche plente grewe there never in mede.
Ful gaye was al the grounde, and queynt
And poudred, as men had it peynt

With many a fresshe and sondrie floure,
That casten up ful good savour.

I wol nat longe holde you in fable
Of al this garden delectable,
I mote my tonge stynten nede;
For I ne maye withouten drede
Naught tellen you the beaute al,
Ne halfe the bounte there with al.

I went on right honde and on lefte
About the place; it was nat lefte
Tyl I had al the garden [in] bene,
In the esters that men myghte sene.
And thus while I wente in my playe
The God of Love me folowed aye,
Right as an hunter can abyde
The beest, tyl he seeth his tyde
To shoten at good messe to the dere,
Whan that hym nedeth go no nere.

And so befyl I rested me
Besydes a wel under a tree,
Whiche tree in Fraunce men cal a pyne;
But sithe the tyme of kyng Pepyne,
Ne grewe there tree in mannes syght
So fayre, ne so wel woxe in hight,
In al that yarde so high was none.
And springyng in a marble stone
Had nature set, the sothe to telle,
Under that pyne tree a welle;
And on the border al withoute
Was written in the stone aboute
Letters smal, that sayden thus:
"Here starfe the fayre Narcisus."

Narcisus was a bachelere
That Love had caught in his daungere,
And in his nette gan hym so strayne,
And dyd him so to wepe and playne,
That nede him must his lyfe forgo.
For a fayre lady that hight Echo
Him loved over any creature,
And gan for hym suche payne endure,
That on a tyme she him tolde
That, if he her loven nolde,
That her behoved nedes dye,
There laye none other remedye.

But nathelesse for his beaute
So feirs and daungerous was he
That he nolde graunte hir askyng,
For wepyng ne for faire praiyng.
And whanne she herd hym werne soo,
She hadde in herte so gret woo,
And took it in so gret dispite,
That she withoute more respite
Was deed anoon. But er she deied
Full pitously to god she preied,
That proude-hertid Narcisus,
That was in love so daungerous,
Myght on a day be hampred so
For love, and ben so hoot for woo,
That never he myght to joye atteyne,
Than he shulde feele in every veyne
What sorowe trewe lovers maken
That ben so velaynesly forsaken.
This prayer was but resonable,
Therfore god helde it ferme and stable.
For Narcisus, shortly to telle,
By aventure come to that welle,
To resten hym in that shadowing
A day whanne he come fro huntyng.
This Narcisus hadde suffred paynes
For rennyng alday in the playnes,
And was for thurst in grete distresse
Of heet, and of his werynesse
That hadde his breth almost bynomen.

LOVE PURSUING

LOVE PURSUING

Whanne he was to that welle y-comen,
That shadowid was with braunches
grene,
He thoughte of thilke water shene
To drynke, and fresshe hym wel withalle;
And doun on knees he gan to falle,
And forth his heed and necke out-straught
To drynken of that welle a draught.
And in the water anoon was sene
His nose, his mouth, his yen shene,
And he therof was all abasshed;
His owne shadowe had hym bytrasshed,
For well wende he the forme see
Of a child of gret beaute.
Well kouthe Love hym wreke thoo
Of daunger and of pride also,
That Narcisus somtyme hym beere.
He quytte hym well his guerdoun there;
For he musede so in the welle
That, shortly all the sothe to telle,
He lovede his owne shadowe soo,
That atte laste he starf for woo.
For whanne he saugh that he his wille
Myght in no maner way fulfille,
And that he was so faste caught
That he hym kouthe comforte nought,
He loste his witte right in that place,
And deyde withynne a lytel space.
And thus his warisoun he took
Fro the lady that he forsook.
Ladyes I preye ensample takith,
Ye that ageyns youre love mistakith;
For if her deth be yow to wite,
God kan ful well youre while quyte.
Whanne that this lettre of which I telle
Hadde taught me that it was the welle
Of Narcisus in his beaute,
I gan anoon withdrawe me,
Whanne it felle in my remembraunce
That hym bitidde such myschaunce.
But at the laste thanne thought I
That scatheles full sykerly
I myght unto the welle goo—
Wherof shulde I abaisshen soo?
Unto the welle than went I me,
And doun I loutede forto see
The clere water in the stoon,
And eke the gravell which that shoon
Down in the botme as silver fyn.
For of the well this is the fyn,
In world is noon so clere of hewe.
The water is evere fresh and newe
That welmeth up with wawis bright
The mountance of two fynger hight.
Abouten it is gras spryngyng
For moiste so thikke and wel likyng,
That it ne may in wynter dye
No more than may the see be drye.

Downe at the botme sette sawe I
Two cristall stonys craftely
In thilke freshe and faire welle.
But o thing sothly dar I telle
That ye wole holde a gret mervayle
Whanne it is tolde, withouten fayle.
For whanne the sonne clere in sight
Cast in that welle his bemys bright,
And that the heete descendid is,
Thanne taketh the cristall stoon y-wis
Agayn the sonne an hundrid hewis,
Blewe, yelowe, and rede that fresh and
newe is
Yitt hath the merveilous cristall
Such strengthe, that the place overall,
Bothe flour, and tree, and leves grene,
And all the yerde in it is seene.
And forto don you to undirstonde,
To make ensample wole I fonde.

Ryght as a myrrour openly
Shewith alle thing that stont therby,
As well the colour as the figure,
Withouten ony coverture ;
Right so the cristall stoon shynyng,
Withouten ony disseyvyng,
The estrees of the yerde accusith,
To hym that in the water musith.
For evere in which half that ye be
Ye may well half the gardyne se ;
And if he turne, he may right well
Sene the remenaunt everydell.
For ther is noon so litil thyng
So hidde ne closid with shittyng,
That it ne is sene as though it were
Peyntid in the cristall there.
This is the mirrour perilous,
In which the proude Narcisus
Sawe all his face faire and bright ;
That made hym swithe to lie upright.
For who so loketh in that mirrour,
Ther may no thyng ben his socour,
That he ne shall there sene some thyng
That shal hym lede into lovyng.
Full many worthy man hath it
Y-blent, for folk of grettist wit
Ben soone caught heere and awayted ;
Withouten respite ben they baited.
Heere comth to folk of newe rage,
Heere chaungith many wight corage ;
Heere lith no rede ne witte therto,
For Venus sone, daun Cupido,
Hath sowen there of love the seed,
That help ne lith there noon, ne rede,
So cerclith it the welle aboute.
His gynnes hath he sett withoute,
Ryght forto cacche in his panters
These damoysels and bachelers.
Love will noon other bridde cacche
Though he sette either nette or lacche.
And for the seed that heere was sowen
This welle is clepid, as well is knowen,
The Welle of Love of verray right,
Of which ther hath ful many a wight
Spoke in bookis dyversely.
But they shull never so verily
Descripcioun of the welle heere,
Ne eke the sothe of this matere,
As ye shull, whanne I have undo
The craft that hir bilongith to.

Allway me liked forto dwelle
To sene the cristall in the welle,
That shewide me full openly
A thousand thinges faste by.
But I may say in sory houre
Stode I to loken or to poure,
For sithen [have] I sore siked ;
That mirrour hath me now entriked.
But hadde I first knowen in my wit
The vertue and [the] strengthe of it,
I nolde not have mused there ;
Me had bette bene ellis where,
For in the snare I fell anoon
That hath bitresshed many oon.
In thilke mirrour sawe I tho,
Among a thousand thinges mo,
A roser chargid full of rosis,
That with an hegge aboute enclos is.
Tho had I sich lust and envie,
That for Parys, ne for Pavie,
Nolde I have left to goon and see
There grettist hepe of roses be.
Whanne I was with this rage hent,
That caught hath many a man and shent,
Toward the roser gan I go.
And whanne I was not fer therfro,
The savour of the roses swote

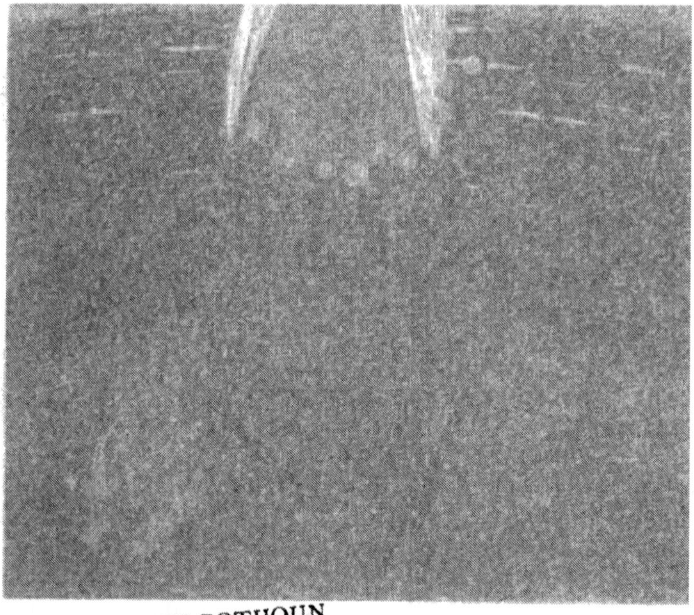

THE BOTHOUN

Ryg[illegible]
She[illegible] therby,
As w[illegible] the figure,
Wi[illegible] coverture ;
Rig[illegible] cristall stoon shynyng,
Wit[illegible] disseyvyng,
Th[illegible] of the yerde accusith
To [illegible] the water musith.
Fo[illegible] which half that ye be
Ye [illegible] half the gardyne se ;
An[illegible], he may right well
Se[illegible] everydell.
F[illegible] so litil thyng
S[illegible] ne closid with shittyng,
That it ne is sene as though it were
Peyntid in the cristall there.
This is the mirrour perilous,
In which the proude Narcisus
Sawe all his face faire and bright ;
That made hym swithe to lie upright.
For who so loketh in that mirrour,
Ther may no thyng ben his socour,
That he ne shall there sene some thyng
That shal hym lede into lovyng.
Full many worthy man hath it
Yblent, for folk of grettist wit
Ben soone caught heere and awayted ;
Withouten respite ben they baited.
Heere comth to folk of newe rage,
Heere chaungith many wight corage ;
Heere lith no rede ne witte therto,
For Venus sone, daun Cupido,
Hath sowen there of love the seed,
That help ne lith there noon, ne rede,
So cerclith it the welle aboute.
His gynnes hath he sett withoute,
Ryght for to cacche in his panters
These damoysels and bachelers.
Love will noon other bridde cacche
Though he sette either nette or lacche.
And for the seed that heere was sowen
This welle is clepid, as well is knowen,
The Welle of Love of verray right,
Of which ther hath ful many a wight
Spoke in bookis dyversely.
But they shull never so verily
Descripcioun of the welle heere,
Ne eke the sothe of this matere,
As ye shull, whanne I have undo
The craft that hir bilongith to.

Allway me liked forto dwelle
To sene the cristall in the welle,
That shewide me full openly
A thousand thinges faste by.
But I may say in sory houre
Stode I to loken or to poure,
For sithen [have] I sore siked ;
That mirrour hath me now entriked.
But hadde I first knowen in my wit
The vertue and [the] strengthe of it,
I nolde not have mused there ;
Me had bettre bene ellis where,
For in the snare I fell anoon
That hath bitresshed many oon.
In thilke mirrour sawe I tho,
Among a thousand thinges mo,
A roser chargid full of rosis,
That with an hegge aboute enclos is.
Tho had I sich lust and envie,
That for Parys, ne for Pavie,
Nolde I have left to goon and see
There grettist hepe of roses be.
Whanne I was with this rage hent,
That caught hath many a man and shent,
Toward the roser gan I go.
And whanne I was not fer therfro,
The savour of the roses swote

Ryg[illegible]
Shew[illegible]
As w[illegible]
With[illegible]
Right [illegible] tall st[illegible]
With[illegible] disc[illegible]
The [illegible] of the [illegible]
To [illegible] ter mouth
For [illegible] that ye be
Ye [illegible] half the gardyne se;
An[illegible] he may right well
Se [illegible] everydell.
For [illegible] so litil thyng
S[illegible] ne closid with shittyng,
That it ne is sene as though it were
Peyntid in the cristall there.
This is the mirrour perilous,
In which the proude Narcisus
Sawe all his face faire and bright;
That made hym swithe to lie upright.
For who so loketh in that mirrour,
Ther may no thyng ben his socour,
That he ne shall there sene some thyng
That sh[illegible] hym lede into lovyng.
Full many worthy man hath it
Y-blent, for folk of grettist wit
Ben soone caught heere and awayted;
Withouten respite ben they baited.
Heere comth to folk of newe rage,
Heere chaungith many wight corage;
Heere lith no rede ne witte therto,
For Venus sone, daun Cupido,
Hath so[illegible] there of love the seed,
That help ne lith there noon, ne rede,
So cerclith it the welle aboute.
His gynnes hath he sett withoute,
Ry[illegible] to cacche in his panters
These damoysels and bachelers.
Love will n[illegible] other bridde cacche
[illegible] hette either nette or lacche.
And [illegible] was sowen
[illegible] knowen,
[illegible] right,
[illegible] ther hath ful many a wight
[illegible] in bookis dyversely.
But they shull never so verily
Descripcioun of the welle heere,
Ne eke the sothe of this matere,
As ye shull, whanne I have undo
The craft that hir bilongith to.

Allway me liked forto dwelle
To sene the cristall in the welle,
That shewide me full openly
A thousand thinges faste by.
But I may say in sory houre
Stode I to loken or to poure,
For sithen [have] I sore siked;
That mirrour hath me now entriked.
But hadde I first knowen in my wit
The vertue and [the] strengthe of it,
I nolde not have mused there;
Me hadde bette bene ellis where,
For in the snare I fell anoon
That hath bitresshed many oon.
In thilke mirrour sawe I tho,
Among a thousand thinges mo,
A roser chargid full of rosis,
That with an hegge aboute enclos is.
Tho had I sich lust and envie,
That for Parys ne for Pavie,
Nolde I have left to goon and see
There grettist hepe of roses be.
Whanne I was with this rage hent,
[illegible] may a man and shent,
Toward [illegible] I go.
And whanne [illegible] ter therfro,
The savour [illegible] swote

Me smote right to the herte rote,
As I hadde all embawmed be.
And if I ne hadde endouted me
To have ben hatid or assailed,
My thankis wolde I not have failed
To pulle a rose of all that route
To beren in myn honde aboute,
And smellen to it where I wente;
But ever I dredde me to repente,
And leste it grevede or forthought
The lord that thilke gardyn wrought.
Of roses ther were grete wone,
So faire waxe never in rone.
Of knoppes clos some sawe I there,
And some wel beter woxen were;
And some ther ben of other moysoun,
That drowe nygh to her sesoun,
And spedde hem faste forto sprede.
I love well sich roses rede,
For brode roses and open also
Ben passed in a day or two,
But knoppes wille [al] freshe be
Two dayes atte leest or thre.
The knoppes gretly liked me,
For fairer may ther no man se.
Who-so myght have oon of all,
It ought hym ben full lief withall;
Might I gerlond of hem geten,
For no richesse I wolde it leten.
Among the knoppes I chese oon
So faire, that of the remenaunt noon
No preise I half so well as it,
Whanne I avise it in my wit.
For it so well was enlumyned
With colour reed, [and] as well fyned
As nature couthe it make faire;
And it hath leves wel foure paire,
That kynde hath sett thorough his knowyng
Aboute the rede roses spryngyng.
The stalke was as rishe right,
And theron stode the knoppe upright,
That it ne bowide upon no side.
The swote smelle spronge so wide,
That it dide all the place aboute.
Whanne I hadde smelled the savour swote,
No will hadde I fro thens yit goo;
Bot somdell neer it wente I thoo
To take it, but myn hond for drede
Ne dorste I to the rose bede
For thesteles sharpe of many maneeres,
Netles, thornes, and hokede breres,
For myche they distourbled me,
That sore I dradde to harmed be.

The God of Love with bowe bent,
That all day sette hadde his talent
To pursuen and to spien me,
Was stondyng by a fige tree.
And whanne he sawe how that I
Hadde chosen so ententifly
The bothoun more unto my paie
Than ony other that I say,
He toke an arowe full sharply whette,
And in his bowe whanne it was sette,
He streight up to his ere drough
The stronge bowe, that was so tough,
And shette att me so wondir smerte,
That thorough myn ye unto myn herte
The takel smote, and depe it wente.
And therwith-all such colde me hente,
That, under clothes warme and softe,
Sithen that day I have chevered ofte.
Whanne I was hurt thus, in [a] stounde
I felle doun platte unto the grounde;
Myn herte failed and feynted ay,
And longe tyme a-swoone I lay.
But whanne I come out of swounyng,

And hadde witt and my felyng,
I was all maate, and wende full well
Of bloode have loren a full gret dell.
But certes the arowe that in me stode
Of me ne drewe no drope of blode,
For why I founde my wounde alldreye.
Thanne toke I with myn hondis tweie
The arowe, and ful fast out it plight,
And in the pullyng sore I sight;
So at the last the shaft of tree
I drough out with the fethers thre
But yet the hokede heed y-wis,
The which that Beaute callid is,
Gan so depe in myn herte pace
That I it myghte nought arace;
But in myn herte still it stode.
Al bledde I not a drope of blode.
I was bothe anguyssous and trouble
For the perill that I sawe double.
I nyste what to seye or do,
Ne gete a leche my woundis to;
For neithir thorough gras ne rote
Ne hadde I helpe of hope ne bote.
But to the bothoun evermo
Myn herte drewe, for all my wo;
My thought was in noon other thing,
For hadde it ben in my kepyng,
It wolde have brought my lyf agayn.
For certis evenly, I dar wel seyn,
The sight oonly and the savour
Alegged mych of my langour.
Thanne gan I forto drawe me
Toward the bothon faire to se.
And Love hadde gete hym in this throwe
Another arowe into his bowe,
And forto shete gan hym dresse;
The arowis name was Symplesse.
And whanne that Love gan nyghe me mere,
He drowe it up withouten were,
And shette at me with all his myght;
So that this arowe anoon right
Thourghout [myn] eigh, as it was founde,
Into myn herte hath maad a wounde.
Thanne I anoon dide al my crafte,
Forto drawen out the shafte;
And therwith-all I sighede efte,
But in myn herte the heed was lefte,
Which ay encreside my desire,
Unto the bothon drawe nere.
And evermo that me was woo,
The more desir hadde I to goo
Unto the roser, where that grewe
The freysshe bothun so bright of hewe.
Betir me were to have laten be,
But it bihovede nede me
To done right as myn herte badde,
For evere the body must be ladde
Aftir the herte, in wele and woo;
Of force togidre they must goo.
But never this archer wolde feyne
To shete at me with all his peyne.
And forto make me to hym mete,
The thridde arowe he gan to shete,
Whanne best his tyme he myght espie,
The which was named Curtesie.
Into myn herte it dide avale.
A-swoone I fell bothe deed and pale,
Long tyme I lay and stired nought,
Till I abraide out of my thought.
And faste thanne I avysede me
To drawe out the shafte of tree;
But evere the heed was left bihynde,
For ought I couthe pulle or wynde.
So sore it stikid whanne I was hit,
That by no craft I myght it flit.
But anguyssous and full of thought
I felt sich woo my wounde ay wrought,

THE THREE ARROWS OF LOVE

thers thre
y-wis,
allid is,
e pace
arace ;
tode.
f blode.
nd trouble
double.
o,
dis to ;
s ne rote
e ne bote.
no
my wo ;
other thing,
epyng,
y lyf agayn.
el seyn,
savour
gour.
e me
to se.
inthisthrowe
owe,
dresse ;
nplesse.

Unto the bothon drawe nere.
And evermo that me was woo,
The more desir hadde I to goo
Unto the roser, where that grewe
The freysshe bothun so bright of hewe.
Betir me were to have laten be,
But it bihovede nede me
To done right as myn herte badde,
For evere the body must be ladde
Aftir the herte, in wele and woo;
Of force togidre they must goo.
But never this archer wolde feyne
To shete at me with all his peyne,
And forto make me to hym mete,
The thridde arowe he gan to shete,
Whanne best his tyme he myght espie,
The which was named Curtesie.
Into myn herte it dide avale.
A-swoone I fell bothe deed and pale,
Long tyme I lay and stired nought,
Till I abraide out of my thought.
And faste thanne I avysede me
To drawe out the shafte of tree;
But evere the heed was left bihynde,
For ought I [illegible] pulle or wynde.
So sore [illegible] I was hit,
That b[illegible]ght it flit.
[illegible] of thought

That somonede me alway to goo
Toward the rose, that plesede me soo.
But I ne durste in no manere,
Bicause the archer was so nere;
"For evermore gladly," as I rede,
"Brent child of fier hath myche drede."
And certis yit, for al my peyne,
Though that I sigh yit arwis reyne,
And grounde quarels sharpe of steele,
Ne for no payne that I myght feele,
Yit myght I not my-silf witholde
The faire roser to biholde.
For Love me yaf sich hardement
Forto fulfille his comaundement,
Upon my fete I rose up thanne,
Feble as a forwoundid man,
And forth to gon [my] myght I sette,
And for the archer nolde I lette.
Toward the roser fast I drowe,
But thornes sharpe mo than ynowe
Ther were, and also thisteles thikke
And breres brymme forto prikke,
That I ne myghte gete grace
The rowe thornes forto passe,
To sene the roses fresshe of hewe.
I must abide, though it me rewe,
The hegge aboute so thikke was,
That closide the roses in compas.
But o thing lyked me right wele;
I was so nygh I myghte fele
Of the bothon the swote odour,
And also se the fresshe colour.
And that right gretly liked me,
That I so neer myght it se.
Sich joie anoon therof hadde I,
That I forgate my maladie;
To sene I hadde siche delit,
Of sorwe and angre I was al quyte,
And of my woundes that I hadde thore.
For no thing liken me myght more
Than dwellen by the roser ay,
And thennes never to passe away
But whanne a while I hadde be thare,
The god of Love, which alto-share
Myn herte with his arwis kene,
Cast hym to yeve me woundis grene.
He shette at me full hastily
An arwe named Company,
The whiche takell is full able
To make these ladies merciable.
Thanne I anoon gan chaungen hewe
For grevaunce of my wounde newe,
That I agayn fell in swounyng,
And sighede sore in compleynyng.
Soore I compleyned that my sore
On me gan greven more and more.
I hadde noon hope of allegeaunce;
So nygh I drowe to desperaunce,
I roughte [ne] of deth ne lyf.
Wheder that Love wolde me dryf,
Yf me a martir wolde he make,
I myght his power nought forsake.
And while for anger thus I woke,
The God of Love an arowe toke;
Ful sharpe it was and [ful] pugnaunt.
And it was callid Faire Semblaunt,
The which in no wise wole consente,
That ony lover hym repente
To serve his love with herte and all
For ony perill that may bifall.
But though this arwe was kene grounde,
As ony rasour that is founde
To kutte and kerve, at the poynt
The God of Love it hadde anoynt
With a precious oynement,
Somdell to yeve aleggement
Upon the woundes that he hadde
Through the body in my herte made,

To helpe her sores and to cure,
And that they may the bette endure.
But yit this arwe, withoute more,
Made in myn herte a large sore,
That in full grete peyne I abode.
But ay the oynement wente abrode,
Thourgh-oute my woundes large & wide
It spredde aboute in every side.
Through whos vertu and whos myght
Myn herte joyfull was and light;
I hadde ben deed and alto-shent
But for the precious oynement.
The shaft I drowe out of the arwe,
Roukyng for wo right wondir narwe,
But the heed, which made me smerte,
Lefte bihynde in myn herte
With other foure, I dar wel say,
That never wole be take away.
But the oynement halpe me wele;
And yit sich sorwe dide I fele
That al day I chaunged hewe
Of my woundes fresshe and newe.
As men myght se in my visage,
The arwis were so full of rage,
So variaunt of diversitee,
That men in everiche myght se
Bothe gret anoy, and eke swetnesse
And joie meynt with bittirnesse.
Now were they esy, now were they wode,
In hem I felte bothe harme and goode;
Now sore without aleggement,
Now softyng with the oynement;
It softed heere and prikked there,
Thus ese and anger to-gidre were.
The God of Love delyverly
Come lepande to me hastily,
And seide to me in gret rape,
"Yelde thee, for thou may not escape,
May no defence availe thee heere;
Therfore I rede make no daungere,
If thou wolt yelde thee hastely.
Thou shalt [the] rather have mercy.
He is a foole in sikernesse,
That with daunger or stoutenesse
Rebellith there that he shulde plese;
In sich folye is litel ese.
Be meke where thou must nedis bowe,
To stryve ageyn is nought thi prowe;
Come at oones and have y-doo,
For I wole that it be soo.
Thanne yelde thee heere debonairly."
And I answerid ful hombly:
"Gladly sir at youre biddyng
I wole me yelde in alle thyng;
To youre servyse I wole me take,
For god defende that I shulde make
Ageyn youre biddyng resistence,
I wole not don so grete offence.
For if I dide, it were no skile;
Ye may do with me what ye wile,
Save or spille and also sloo.
Fro you in no wise may I goo,
My lyf, my deth is in youre honde,
I may not laste out of youre bonde;
Pleyn at youre lyst I yelde me,
Hopyng in herte that sumtyme ye
Comfort and ese shull me sende,
Or ellis shortly, this is the eende,
Withouten helthe I mote ay dure,
But if ye take me to youre cure.
Comfort or helthe how shuld I have,
Sith ye me hurt, but ye me save?
The helthe of love mot be founde
Where as they token firste her wounde.
And if ye lyst of me to make
Youre prisoner, I wole it take
Of herte and willfully at gree;
Hoolly and pleyn y yelde me,

Withoute feynyng or feyntise,
To be governed by youre emprise.
Of you I here so mych pris,
I wole ben hool at youre devis
Forto fulfille youre lykyng,
And repente for no thyng,
Hopyng to have yit in some tide
The mercy of that I abide."
And with that covenaunt yelde I me,
Anoon down knelyng upon my kne,
Proferyng forto kisse his feete.
But for no thyng he wolde me lete,
And seide, "I love thee bothe and preise,
Sens that thyn answer doth me ese,
For thou answerid so curteisly.
For now I wote wel uttirly
That thou art gentyll by thi speche;
For, though a man fer wolde seche,
He shulde not fynden in certeyn
No sich answer of no vileyn,
For sich a word ne myghte nought
Isse out of a vilayns thought.
Thou shalt not lesen of thi speche,
For [to] thy helpyng wole I eche,
And eke encresen that I may.
But first I wole that thou obaye
Fully for thyn avauntage,
Anoon to do me heere homage;
And sithe kisse thou shalt my mouthe,
Which to no vilayn was never couthe
Forto aproche it ne forto touche.
For sauff of cherlis I ne vouche
That they shull never neigh it nere;
For curteis and of faire manere,
Well taught and full of gentilnesse,
He muste ben that shal me kysse;
And also of full high fraunchise,
That shal atteyne to that emprise.
And first of o thing warne I thee,
That peyne and gret adversite
He mote endure, and eke travaile,
That shal me serve withoute faile.
But ther ageyns thee to comforte,
And with thi servise to desporte,
Thou mayst full glad and joyfull be
So good a maister to have as me,
And lord of so high renoun.
I bere of love the gonfenoun,
Of curtesie the banere.
For I am of the silf manere,
Gentil, curteys, meke, and fre,
That who ever ententyf be
Me to honoure, doute, and serve,
Nede is that he hym observe
Fro trespasse and fro vilanye,
And hym governe in curtesie
With will and with entencioun.
For whanne he first in my prisoun
Is caught, thanne must be uttirly
Fro thennes forth full bisily
Caste hym gentyll forto bee
If he desire helpe of me."
Anoon withoute more delay,
Withouten daunger or affray,
I bicome his man anoon,
And gave hym thankes many a oon,
And knelide doun with hondis joynt,
And made it in my port full quoint.
The joye wente to myn herte rote,
Whanne I hadde kissed his mouth so swote;
I hadde sich myrthe and sich likyng
It cured me of langwisshing.
He askide of me thanne hostages.
"I have," he seide, "taken fele homages
Of oon and other, where I have bene
Disceyved ofte withouten wene.
These felouns full of falsite

Have many sithes biguyled me,
And through falshede her lust achieved,
Whereof I repente and am agreved.
And I hem gete in my daungere,
Her falshede shull they bie full dere!
But for I love thee, I seie thee pleyn,
I wole of thee be more certeyn.
For thee so sore I wole now bynde,
That thou away ne shalt not wynde
Forto denyen the covenaunt
Or don that is not avenaunt.
That thou were fals it were gret reuthe,
Sith thou semest so full of treuthe."
"Sire, if thee lyst to undirstande,
I merveile the askyng this demande.
For why or wherfore shulde ye
Ostages, or borwis aske of me,
Or ony other sikirnesse,
Sith ye wote in sothfastnesse
That ye have me susprised so,
And hole myn herte taken me fro,
That it wole do for me no thing
But if it be at youre biddyng;
Myn herte is youres and myn right nought
As it bihoveth in dede and thought,
Redy in all to worche youre will,
Whether so turne to good or ill.
So sore it lustith you to plese,
No man therof may you desese.
Ye have theron sette sich justice,
That it is werreid in many wise.
And if ye doute it nolde obeye,
Ye may therof do make a keye,
And holde it with you for ostage."
"Now certis this is noon outrage,"
Quod Love, "and fully I acorde;
For of the body he is full lord
That hath the herte in his tresour;
Outrage it were to asken more."
Thanne of his awmener he drough
A litell keye, fetys ynowgh,
Which was of gold polisshed clere;
And seide to me, "With this keye heere
Thyn herte to me now wole I shette;
For all my jowell, loke and knette,
I bynde undir this litel keye,
That no wight may carie aweye.
This keye is full of gret poste."
With which anoon he touchide me
Under the side full softily,
That he myn herte sodeynly
Without anoye hadde spered,
That yit right nought it hath me dered.
Whanne he hadde don his will al oute,
And I hadde putte hym out of doute,
"Sire," I seide, "I have right gret wille
Youre lust and plesaunce to fulfille.
Loke ye my servise take atte gree
By thilke feith ye owe to me.
I seye nought for recreaundise,
For I nought doute of youre servise,
But the servaunt traveileth in vayne,
That forto serven doth his payne
Unto that lord which in no wise
Kan hym no thank for his servyse."
Love seide, "Dismaie thee nought,
Syn thou for sokour hast me sought;
In thank thi servise wole I take
And high of gre I wole thee make,
If wikkidnesse ne hyndre thee;
But as I hope it shal nought be,
To worshipe no wight by aventure
May come, but if he peyne endure;
Abide and suffre thy distresse
That hurtith now; it shal be lesse.
I wote my silf what may thee save,
What medicyne thou woldist have;
And if thi trouthe to me thou kepe,

I shal unto thyn helpyng eke,
To cure thy woundes and make hem clene,
Where so they be olde or grene;
Thou shalt be holpen at wordis fewe.
For certeynly thou shalt well shewe
Where that thou servest with good wille
Forto accomplysshen and fulfille
My comaundementis day and nyght
Whiche I to lovers yeve of right."
'Ah Sire, for goddis love," seide I,
'Er ye passe hens ententyfly,
Youre comaundementis to me ye say,
And I shall kepe hem if I may.
For hem to kepen is all my thought
And if so be I wote hem nought,
Thanne may I [erre] unwityngly.
Wherfore I pray you entierly,
With all myn herte me to lere,
That I trespasse in no manere."
The God of Love thanne chargide me,
Anoon as ye shall here and see,
Worde by worde by right emprise,
So as the Romance shall devise.
The maister lesith his tyme to lere
Whanne the disciple wole not here;
It is but veyn on hym to swynke
That on his lernyng wole not thynke.
Who so luste love, late hym entende,
For now the Romance bigynneth to
amende,
Now is good to here in fay
If ony be that can it say,
And poynte it as the resoun is.
Set forth [an] other gate ywys,
It shall nought well in alle thyng
Be brought to good undirstondyng.
For a reder that poyntith ille
A good sentence may ofte spille.
The book is good at the eendyng
Maad of newe and lusty thyng
For who so wole the eendyng here,
The crafte of love he shall mowe lere,
If that ye wole so long abide
Tyl I this Romance may unhide,
And undo the signifiance
Of this dreme into Romance.
The sothfastnesse that now is hidde
Without coverture shall be kidde,
Whanne I undon have this dremyng,
Wherynne no word is of lesyng.

"Vylanye at the bigynnyng
I wole," sayde Love, "over alle thyng
Thou leve, if thou wolt nought be
Fals and trespasse ageyns me.
I curse and blame generaly
All hem that loven vilanye.
For vilanye makith vilayn,
And by his dedis a cherle is seyn.
Thise vilayns arn withouten pitee,
Frendshipe, love, and all bounte.
I nyl resseyve unto my servise
Hem that ben vilayns of emprise.
But undirstonde in thyn entent
That this is not myn entendement,
To clepe no wight in noo ages
Oonly gentill for his lynages.
But who so [that] is vertuous,
And in his port nought outrageous,
Whanne sich oon thou seest thee biforn,
Though he be not gentill born,
Thou maist well seyn this is in soth,
That he is gentil by cause he doth
As longeth to a gentilman,
Of hym noon other deme I can.
For certeynly withouten drede
A cherle is demed by his dede
Of hie or lowe, as ye may see,

Or of what kynrede that he bee.
Ne say nought, for noon yvel wille,
Thyng that is to holden stille;
It is no worshipe to mysseye,
Thou maist ensample take of Keye,
That was somtyme, for mysseiyng,
Hated bothe of olde and ying.
As fer as Gaweyn the worthy
Was preised for his curtesie,
Kay was hated, for he was fell,
Of word dispitous and cruell.
Wherfore be wise and aqueyntable,
Goodly of word and resonable,
Bothe to lesse and eke to mare.
And whanne thou comest there men are,
Loke that thou have in custome ay
First to salue hym, if thou may;
And if it fall that of hem somme
Salue thee first, be not domme,
But quyte hym curteisly anoon,
Without abidyng, er they goon.
For no thyng eke thy tunge applye
To speke wordis of rebaudrye;
To vilayne speche in no degre
Late never thi lippe unbounden be,
For I nought holde hym, in good feith,
Curteys that foule wordis seith.
And alle wymmen serve and preise,
And to thy power her honour reise;
And if that ony myssaiere
Dispise wymmen, that thou maist here,
Blame hym and bidde hym holde hym stille.
And set thy myght, and all thy wille,
Wymmen and ladies forto please,
And to do thyng that may hem ese,
That they ever speke good of thee;
For so thou maist best preised be.
Loke fro pride thou kepe thee wele,
For thou maist bothe perceyve and fele,
That pride is bothe foly and synne.
And he that pride hath hym withynne,
Ne may his herte in no wise
Meken ne souplen to servyse.
For pride is founde in every part
Contrarie unto loves art,
And he that loveth trew[e]ly
Shulde hym contene jolily
Withoute pride in sondry wise,
And hym disgysen in queyntise;
For queynte array withoute drede
Is no thyng proude, who takith hede;
For fresh array, as men may see,
Withoute pride may ofte be.
Mayntene thy silf aftir thi rent,
Of robe and eke of garnement;
For many sithe faire clothyng
A man amendith in mych thyng.
And loke alwey that they be shape,
What garnement that thou shalt make,
Of hym that kan [hem] beste do
With all that perteyneth therto.
Poyntis and sleves be well sittande,
Right and streght on the hande;
Of shone and bootes newe and faire,
Loke at the leest thou have a paire,
And that they sitte so fetisly,
That these ruyde may uttirly
Merveyle, sith that they sitte so pleyn,
How they come on or off ageyn.
Were streite gloves with awmere
Of silk, and alwey with good chere
Thou yeve, if thou have [gret] richesse;
And if thou have nought, spende the lesse.
Alwey be mery, if thou may,
But waste not thi good alway.
Have hatte of floures as fresh as May,
Chapelett of roses of Wissonday;

For sich array ne costneth but lite.
Thyn hondis wasshe, thy teeth make
white,
And lete no filthe upon thee bee;
Thy nailes blak if thou maist see,
Voide it awey delyverly;
And kembe thyn heed right jolily.
Farce not thi visage in no wise,
For that of love is not themprise,
For love doth haten, as I fynde,
A beaute that cometh not of kynde.
Alwey in herte, I rede thee,
Glad and mery forto be;
And be as joyfull as thou can,
Love hath no joye of sorowful man.
That yvell is full of curtesie
That lowith in his maladie.
For ever of love the sikenesse
Is meynde with swete and bitternesse.
The sore of love is merveilous,
For now [is] the lover joyous,
Now can he pleyne, now can he grone,
Now can he syngen, now maken mone;
To day he pleyneth for hevynesse,
To morowe he pleyeth for jolynesse.
The lyf of love is full contrarie,
Which stounde-mele can ofte varie.
But if thou canst mirthis make,
That men in gre wole gladly take,
Do it goodly, I comaunde thee.
For men shulde, where so evere they be,
Do thing that [to] hem sittyng is;
For therof cometh good loos and pris.
Where-of that thou be vertuous
Ne be not straunge ne daungerous,
For if that thou good ridere be,
Prike gladly that men may [the] se.
In armes also, if thou konne,
Pursue tyl thou a name hast wonne.
And if thi voice be faire and clere
Thou shalt make [no] gret daungere
Whanne to synge they goodly prey,
It is thi worship fortobeye.
Also to you it longith ay
To harpe and gitterne, daunce and play;
For if he can wel foote and daunce,
It may hym greetly do avaunce.
Among eke, for thy lady sake.
Songes and complayntes [se] that thou
make,
For that wole meven in her herte,
Whanne they reden of thy smerte.
Loke that no man for scarce thee holde,
For that may greve thee many folde;
Resoun wole that a lover be
In his yiftes more large and fre
Than cherles that kan naught of lovyng.
For who therof can ony thyng,
He shall be leef ay forto yeve,
In loves lore who so wolde leve.
For he that through a sodeyn sight,
Or for a kyssyng, anoon right
Yaff hoole his herte in will and thought,
And to hym silf kepith right nought,
Aftir swich gift is good resoun
He yeve his good [al] in abandoun.

Now wole I shortly heere reherce
Of that I have seid in verce
Al the sentence by and by,
In wordis fewe compendiously,
That thou the bet mayst on hem thynke,
Whether so it be thou wake or wynke.
For the wordis litel greve
A man to kepe, whanne it is breve.
Who so with love wole goon or ride,
He mote be curteis and voide of pride,
Mery, and full of jolite,

And of largesse alosed be.
Firste I joyne thee heere in penaunce
That evere, withoute repentaunce,
Thou sette thy thought in thy lovyng
To laste withoute repentyng,
And thenke upon thi myrthis swete,
That shall folowe aftir, whan ye mete.
And for thou trewe to love shalt be,
I wole, and comaunde thee
That in oo place thou sette all hoole
Thyn herte, withoute halfen doole
Of trecherie and sikernesse;
For I lovede nevere doublenesse.
To many his herte that wole departe,
Everiche shal have but litel parte;
But of hym drede I me right nought
That in oo place settith his thought.
Therfore in oo place it sette,
And lat it nevere thennys flette.
For if thou yevest it in lenyng,
I holde it but a wrecchid thyng.
Therfore yeve it hoole and quyte,
And thou shalt have the more merite;
If it be lent, that aftir soone
The bounte and the thank is doone,
But in love fre yeven thing
Requyrith a gret guerdonyng.
Yeve it in yift al quyte fully,
And make thi yifte debonairly,
For men that yifte holde more dere
That yeven [is] with gladsome chere.
That yifte nought to preisen is
That man yeveth maugre his.
Whanne thou hast yeven thyn herte, as I
Have seid [to] thee heere openly,
Thanne aventures shull thee fall
Which harde and hevy ben with-all.
For ofte, whan thou bithenkist thee
Of thy lovyng, where so thou be,
Fro folk thou must departe in hie,
That noon perceyve thi maladie.
But hyde thyne harme thou must alone,
And go forthe sole, and make thy mone.
Thou shalte no whyle be in o state,
But whylom colde and whilom hate,
Now reed as rose, now yelowe and fade.
Suche sorowe I trowe thou never hade;
Cotidien, ne quarteyne,
It is nat so ful of peyne.
For often tymes it shal fal
In love, among thy paynes al,
That thou thy selfe al holy
Foryeten shalte so utterly,
That many tymes thou shalte be
Styl as an ymage of tree,
Domme as a stone, without steryng
Of fote or honde, without spekyng.

Than, soone after al thy payne,
To memorye shalte thou come agayne,
A man abasshed wonder sore,
And after syghen more and more.
For wytte thou wele, withouten wene,
In suche astate ful ofte have bene,
That have the yvel of love assayde,
Wherthrough thou arte so dismayde.
After a thought shal take the so,
That thy love is to ferre the fro;
Thou shalte saye 'God! What may this be
That I ne maye my lady se?
Myne herte alone is to her go,
And I abyde al sole in wo,
Departed fro myne owne thought,
And with myne eyen se right nought.

Alas! myne eyen send I ne may
My careful herte to convay!
Myne hertes gyde but they be,

I prayse nothyng what ever they se.
Shul they abyde than? nay,
But gone visyte without delay,
That myne herte desyreth so.
For certainly, but if they go,
A foole my selfe I maye wel holde,
Whan I ne se what myne hert wolde.
Wherfore I wol gone her to sene,
For eased shal I never bene,
But I have some tokenyng.'

Than gost thou forthe without dwellyng.
But ofte thou faylest of thy desyre,
Er thou mayst come her any nere,
And wastest in vayn thi passage.
Thanne fallest thou in a newe rage;
For want of sight, thou gynnest morne,
And homewarde pensyf thou dost retorne.
In greet myscheef thanne shalt thou bee,
For thanne agayne shall come to thee
Sighes and pleyntes with newe woo,
That no yecchyng prikketh soo.
Who wote it nought, he may go lere
Of hem that bien love so dere.
No thyng thyn herte appesen may
That ofte thou wole goon and assay,
If thou maist seen by aventure
Thi lyves joy, thine hertis cure.
So that bi grace if thou myght
Atteyne of hire to have a sight,
Thanne shalt thou done noon other dede,
But with that sight thyne eyen fede.
That faire fresh whanne thou maist see,
Thyne herte shall so ravysshed be,
That nevere thou woldest, thi thankis, lete
Ne remove forto see that swete.
The more thou seest, in sothfastnesse,
The more thou coveytest of that swetnesse;
The more thine herte brenneth in fier,
The more thine herte is in desire.
For who considreth everydeell,
It may be likned wondir well
The peyne of love unto a fere.
For evermore thou neighest nere,
Thou or whoo so that it bee,
For verray sothe I tell it thee,
The hatter evere shall thou brenne,
As experience shall thee kenne.
Where so comest in ony coost,
Who is next fuyre he brenneth moost.
And yitt forsothe for all thine hete,
Though thou for love swelte and swete,
Ne for no thyng thou felen may,
Thou shalt not willen to passen away.
And though thou go, yitt must thee nede
Thenke alle day on hir fairhede,
Whom thou biheelde with so good wille,
And holde thi silf biguyled ille
That thou ne haddest noon hardement
To shewe hir ought of thyne entent.
Thyn herte full sore thou wolt dispise,
And eke repreve of cowardise,
That thou, so dulle in every thing,
Were domme for drede withoute spekyng.
Thou shalt eke thenke thou didest folye,
That thou were hir so faste bye,
And durst not auntre thee to say
Som thyng er thou cam away.
For thou haddist nomore wonne,
To speke of hir whanne thou bigonne,
But yitt she wolde, for thy sake,
In armes goodly thee have take,
It shulde have be more worth to thee
Than of tresour gret plente.
Thus shalt thou morne and eke compleyne,
And gete enchesoun to goone ageyne

Unto the walke, or to the place
Where thou biheelde hir fleshly face.
And never, for fals suspeccioun,
Thou woldest fynde occasioun
Forto gone unto hire hous.
So art thou thanne desirous
A sight of hir forto have,
If thou thine honour myghtist save,
Or ony erande myghtist make,
Thider for thi loves sake
Full fayn thou woldist, but for drede
Thou gost not, lest that men take hede.
Wherfore I red [the] in thi goyng
And also in thyne ageyn comyng,
Thou be well ware that men ne wite;
Feyne thee other cause than itte
To go that weye or faste bye;
To hele wel is no folye.
And if so be it happe thee,
That thou thi love there maist see,
In siker wise thou hir salewe,
Wherewith thi colour wole transmewe,
And eke thy blode shal alto quake,
Thyne hewe eke chaungen for hir sake;
But word and witte with chere full pale
Shull wante [the] forto tell thy tale.
And if thou maist so fer forth wynne,
That thou [thi] resoun dorst bigynne,
And woldist seyn thre thingis or mo,
Thou shalt full scarsly seyn the two.
Though thou bithenke thee never so well,
Thou shalt foryete yit somdell,
But if thou dele with trecherie;
For fals lovers mowe all folye
Seyn what hem lust withouten drede,
They be so double in her falshede;
For they in herte cunne thenke a thyng,
And seyn another in her spekyng.
And whanne thi speche is eendid all,
Ryght thus to thee it shall byfall,
If ony word thanne come to mynde
That thou to seye hast left bihynde.
Thanne thou shalt brenne in gret martire,
For thou shalt brenne as ony fiere,
This is the stryf and eke the affray,
And the batell that lastith ay;
This bargeyn eende may never take,
But if that she thi pees will make.
And whanne the nyght is comen anoon,
A thousande angres shall come uppon.
To bedde as fast thou wolt thee dight,
Where thou shalt have but smal delite;
For whanne thou wenest forto slepe
So full of peyne shalt thou crepe,
Sterte in thi bedde aboute full wide,
And turne full ofte on every side,
Now dounward groff and now upright,
And walowe in woo the longe nyght;
Thine armys shalt thou sprede abrede
As man in werre were forwerede.
Thanne shall thee come a remembraunce
Of hir shappe and hir semblaunce,
Whereto none other may be pere.
And wite thou wel withoute were,
That thee shal [seme] somtyme that nyght
That thou hast hir, that is so bright,
Naked bitwene thyne armes there,
All sothfastnesse as though it were.
Thou shalt make castels thanne in Spayne
And dreme of joye, all but in vayne,
And thee deliten of right nought,
While thou so slomrest in that thought,
That is so swete and delitable;
The which in soth[e] nys but fable,
For it ne shall no while laste.
Thanne shalt thou sighe and wepe faste
And say, 'Dere god, what thing is this?

My dreme is turned all amys,
Which was full swete and apparent;
But now I wake, it is al shent!
How yede this mery thought away!
Twenty tymes upon a day
I wolde this thought wolde come ageyne,
For it aleggith well my peyne;
It makith me full of joyfull thought.
It sleth me that it lastith noght
A lord, why nyl ye me socoure
Fro joye? I trowe that I langoure;
The deth I wolde me shulde sloo
While I lye in hir armes twoo.
Myne harme is harde, withouten wene,
My gret unease full ofte I meene.
But wolde love do so I myght
Have fully joye of hir so bright,
My peyne were quytte me rychely.
Allas, to grete a thing aske I!
Hit is but foly and wrong wenyng
To aske so outrageous a thyng;
And who so askith folily,
He mote be warned hastily.
And I ne wote what I may say,
am so fer out of the way.
For I wolde have full gret likyng
And full gret joye of lasse thing;
For wolde she of hir gentylnesse
Withoute more me oonys kysse,
t were to me a grete guerdoun,
Relees of all my passioun.
But it is harde to come therto,
All is but folye that I do;
So high I have myne herte sette
Where I may no comfort gette;
not where I seye well or nought,
But this I wote wel in my thought,
That it were better of hir alloone,
Forto stynte my woo and moone,
A loke on me I-caste goodly,
Than forto have al utterly
Of an other all hoole the pley.
A lord, where I shall byde the day
That evere she shall my lady be?
He is full cured that may hir see.
A god, whanne shal the dawnyng
springe?
To lye thus is an angry thyng;
I have no joye thus heere to lye
Whanne that my love is not me bye.
A man to lye hath gret disese,
Which may not slepe ne reste in ese.
I wolde it dawed and were now day,
And that the nyght were went away;
For were it day I wolde uprise.
A slowe sonne, shewe thine enprise!
Spede thee to sprede thy beemys bright,
And chace the derknesse of the nyght,
To putte away the stoundes stronge,
Whiche in me lasten all to longe!'
The nyght shalt thou contene soo
Withoute rest, in peyne and woo.
If evere thou knewe of love distresse,
Thou shalt mowe lerne in that sicknesse,
And thus enduryng shalt thou lye,
And ryse on morwe up erly
Out of thy bedde, and harneyse thee,
Er evere dawnyng thou maist see.
All pryvyly thanne shall thou goon,
What weder it be, thi silf alloon,
For reyne or hayle, for snowe, for slete,
Thider she dwellith that is so swete.
The which may fall a-slepe be,
And thenkith but lytel upon thee
Thanne shalt thou goon ful foule a-feerd
Loke if the gate be unspered,
And waite without in woo and peyne,
Full yvel acoolde, in wynde and reyne.

Thanne shal thou go the dore bifore,
If thou maist fynde ony score,
Or hoole, or reeft what evere it were.
Thanne shalt thou stoupe, and lay to ere,
If they withynne a-slepe be—
I mene all save the lady free.
Whom wakyng if thou maist aspie,
Go putte thi-silf in jupartie,
To aske grace, and thee bimene,
That she may wite withoute wene
That thou [a-]nyght no rest hast hadde,
So sore for hir thou were bystadde;
Wommen wel ought pite to take
Of hem that sorwen for her sake.
And loke, for love of that relyke,
That thou thenke noon other lyke;
For whanne thou hast so gret annoy,
Shall kysse thee er thou go away,
And holde that in full gret deynte.
And for that noman shal thee see
Bifore the hous, ne in the way,
Loke thou be goone ageyn er day.

Such comyng and such goyng,
Such hevynesse and such wakyng
Makith lovers, withouten wene,
Under her clothes pale and lene.
For love leveth colour ne cleernesse,
Who loveth trewe hath no fatnesse;
Thou shalt wel by thy-silf [y-]see
That thou must nedis assaied be;
For men that shape hem other weye
Falsly her ladyes to bitraye,
It is no wonder though they be fatt,
With false othes her loves they gatt.
For oft I see suche losengours
Fatter than abbatis or priours.
Yit with o thing I thee charge,
That is to seye that thou be large
Unto the mayde that hir doith serve,
So best hir thanke thou shalt deserve.
Yeve hir yiftes, and gete hir grace,
For so thou may thank purchace,
That she thee worthy holde and free,
Thi lady, and all that may thee see.
Also hir servauntes worshipe ay,
And please as mych as thou may;
Grete good through hem may come to the
Bi-cause with hir they ben pryve;
They shal hir telle hoe they thee fande
Curteis, and wys, and well doande,
And she shall preise well the mare.
Loke oute of londe thou be not fare,
And if such cause thou have that thee
Bihoveth to gone out of contree,
Leve hoole thin herte in hostage,
Till thou ageyn make thi passage.
Thenke longe to see the swete thyng,
That hath thine herte in hir kepyng.
Now have I tolde thee in what wise
A lovere shall do me servise;
Do it thanne if thou wolt have
The meede that thou aftir crave."
Whanne Love all this hadde boden me,
I seide hym, "Sire, how may it be
That lovers may in such manere
Endure the peyne ye have seid heere?
I merveyle me wonder faste
How ony man may lyve or laste
In such peyne and [in] such brennyng;
In sorwe and thought, and such sighing,
Aye unrelesed woo to make,
Whether so it be they slepe or wake,
In such annoy contynuely,
As helpe me god, this merveile I
How man, but he were maad of stele,
Myght lyve a monthe such peynes to
fele."

The God of Love thanne seide me,
"Freend, by the feith I owe to thee,
May no man have good but he it bye;
A man loveth more tendirly
The thyng that he hath bought most dere.
For wite thou well, withouten were,
In thanke that thyng is taken more
For which a man hath suffred sore.
Certis no wo ne may atteyne
Unto the sore of loves peyne;
Noon yvel therto ne may amounte,
Nomore than a man [may] counte
The dropes that of the water be.
For drye as well the greete see
Thou myghtist, as the harmes telle
Of hem that with love dwelle
In servyse; for peyne hem sleeth,
And yet ech man wolde fle the deeth.
And trowe thei shulde nevere escape,
Nere that hope couthe hem make
Glad, as man in prisoun sett,
And may not geten forto ete
But barly breed and watir pure,
And lyeth in vermyn and in ordure;
With all this yitt can he lyve,
Good hope such comfort hath hym yive,
Which maketh wene that he shall be
Delyvered and come to liberte.
In fortune is [his] full trust,
Though he lye in strawe or dust;
In hoope is all his susteynyng.
And so for lovers in her wenyng,
Which Love hath shitte in his prisoun,
Good hope is her salvacioun.
Good hope how sore that they smerte
Yeveth hem bothe will and herte
To profre her body to martire;
For hope so sore doith hem desire
To suffre ech harme that men devise
For joye that aftirward shall aryse.
Hope in desire hathe victorie,
In hope of love is all the glorie,
For hope is all that love may yive;
Nere hope ther shulde no lover lyve.
Blessid be hope, which with desire
Avaunceth lovers in such manere!
Good hope is curteis forto please,
To kepe lovers from all disese;
Hope kepith his bonde, and wole abide
For ony perill that may betyde;
For hope to lovers, as most cheef,
Doth hem endure all myscheef;
Hope is her helpe whanne myster is.

And I shall yeve thee eke I-wys
Three other thingis, that gret solas
Doith to hem that be in my las.
The firste good that may be founde
To hem that in my lace be bounde
Is Swete Thought, forto recorde
Thing wherwith thou canst accorde
Best in thyne herte, where she be.
Thenkyng in absence is good to thee.
Whanne ony lover doth compleyne,
And lyveth in distresse and in peyne,
Thanne Swete-Thought shal come as blyve
Awey his angre forto dryve.
It makith lovers to have remembraunce,
Of comfort and of high plesaunce,
That hope hath hight hym forto wynne.
For Thought anoon thanne shall bygynne,
As ferre, god wote, as he can fynde,
To make a mirrour of his mynde;
Forto biholde he wole not lette.
Hir persone he shall afore hym sette,
Hir laughing eyen, persaunt and clere,
Hir shappe, hir fourme, hir goodly chere;
Hir mouth, that is so gracious,

So swete and eke so saverous;
Of all hir fetures he shall take heede,
His eyen with all hir lymes fede.
Thus Swete-Thenkyng shall aswage
The peyne of lovers and her rage.
Thi joye shall double withoute gesse
Whanne thou thenkist on hir semlynesse,
Or of hir laughing, or of hir chere
That to thee made thi lady dere.
This comfort wole I that thou take;
And if the next thou wolt forsake,
Which is not lesse saverous,
Thou shuldist ben to daungerous.

The secounde shal be Swete-speche,
That hath to many oon be leche
To bringe hem out of woo and were,
And holpe many a bachilere,
And many a lady sent socoure,
That have loved paramour,
Through spekyng whanne they myght heere
Of hir lovers, to hem so dere.
To hem it voidith all her smerte,
The which is closed in her herte;
In herte it makith hem glad and light,
Speche, whanne they mowe have [no] sight.
And therfore now it cometh to mynde
In olde dawes, as I fynde,
That clerkis writen that hir knewe;
Ther was a lady, fresh of hewe,
Which of hir love made a songe,
On hym forto remembre amonge,
In which she seyde: 'Whanne that I here
Speken of hym that is so dere,
To me it voidith alle smerte.
I-wys, he sittith so nere myne herte
To speke of hym at eve or morwe
It cureth me of all my sorwe.
To me is noon so high plesaunce
As of his persone dalyaunce.'
She wist full well that Swete-Spekyng
Comfortith in full myche thyng.
Hir love she hadde full well assaid,
Of him she was full well apaid;
To speke of hym hir joye was sett.
Therfore I rede thee that thou gett
A felowe that can well concele,
And kepe thi counsell, and well hele,
To whom go shewe hoolly thine herte,
Bothe well and woo, joye and smerte;
To gete comfort to hym thou goo,
And pryvyly bitwene yow twoo
Yee shall speke of that goodly thyng,
That hath thyne herte in hir kepyng.
Of hir beaute, and hir semblaunce,
And of hir goodly countenaunce;
Of all thi state, thou shalt hym seye,
And aske hym counseill how thou may
Do ony thyng that may hir plese;
For it to thee shall do gret ese,
That he may wite thou trust hym soo,
Bothe of thi wele and of thi woo.
And if his herte to love be sett,
His companye is myche the bett,
For resoun wole he shewe to thee
All uttirly his pryvyte,
And what she is he loveth so.
To thee pleynly he shall undo,
Withoute drede of ony shame,
Bothe tell hir renoun and hir name.
Thanne shall he forther, ferre and nere,
And namely to thi lady dere.
In syker wise yee every other
Shall helpen, as his owne brother,
In trouthe withoute doublenesse,
And kepen cloos in sikernesse;
For it is noble thing in fay

To have a man thou darst say
Thy pryve counsell every deell;
For that wole comforte thee right well,
And thou shalt holde thee well apayed,
Whanne such a freend thou hast assayed.

The thridde good of gret comforte,
That yeveth to lovers moste disporte,
Comyth of sight and of biholdyng,
That clepid is SWETE-LOKYNG.
The which may [thee] noon ese do
Whanne thou art fer thy lady fro.
Wherfore thou prese alwey to be
In place where thou maist hir see.
For it is thyng most amerous,
Most delytable and saverous,
Forto a-swage a mannes sorowe,
To sene his lady by the morwe.
For it is a full noble thing,
Whanne thyne eyen have metyng
With that relike precious
Wherof they be so desirous.
But al day after, soth it is,
They have no drede to faren amysse;
They dreden neither wynde ne reyne,
Ne noon other maner peyne.
For whanne thyne eyen were thus in blisse,
Yit of hir curtesie, y-wysse,
Alloone they can not have her joye,
But to the herte they [it] convoye;
Parte of her blisse to hym they sende,
Of all this harme to make an ende.
The eye is a good messangere,
Which can to the herte in such manere
Tidyngis sende, that hath sene
To voide hym of his peynes clene.
Wherof the herte rejoiseth soo,
That a gret partye of his woo
Is voided, and putte awey to flight,
Right as the derknesse of the nyght
Is chased with clerenesse of the mone,
Right so is al his woo full soone
Devoided clene, whanne that the sight
Biholden may that freshe wight
That the herte desireth soo,
That al his derknesse is agoo.
For thanne the herte is all at ese,
Whanne the eyen sene that may hem plese.
Now have I declared thee all oute
Of that thou were in drede and doute,
For I have tolde thee feithfully
What thee may curen utterly.
And alle lovers that wole be
Feithfull and full of stabilite,
Good hope alwey kepe bi thi side,
And Swete-Thought, make eke abide;
Swete-Lokyng and Swete-Speche.
Of all thyne harmes thei shall be leche:
Of every thou shalt have gret plesaunce,
If thou canst bide in suffraunce,
And serve wel withoute feyntise;
Thou shalt be quyte of thyne emprise
With more guerdoun, if that thou lyve,
But at this tyme this I thee yive."
The God of Love, whanne al the day
Had taught me as ye have herd say,
And enfourmed compendiously,
He vanyshide awey all sodeynly;
And I alloone lefte all soole,
So full of compleynt and of doole,
For I sawe no man there me by.
My woundes me greved wondirly;
Me forto curen no thyng I knewe
Save the bothon bright of hewe,
Wheron was sett hoolly my thought.
Of other comfort knewe I nought,
But it were thrugh the God of Love.

I knewe not elles to my bihove
That myght me ease or comfort gete,
But if he wolde hym entermete.
The roser was withoute doute
Closed with an haye withoute,
As ye toforn have herd me seyne.
And fast I bisiede, and wolde fayne
Have passed the hay, if [that] I myght
Have geten ynne by ony slight
Unto the bothon so faire to see.
But evere I dradde blamed to be,
If men wolde have suspeccioun
That I wolde of entencioun
Have stole the roses that there were;
Therfore to entre I was in fere.
But at the last, as I bithought,
Whether I shulde passe or nought,
I sawe come with a glad chere
To me a lusty bachelere,
Of good stature and of good hight;
And BIALACOIL forsothe he hight,
Sone he was to Curtesie.
And he me grauntide full gladly
The passage of the outter hay,
And seide, "Sir, how that yee may
Passe, if [that] youre wille be
The freshe roser forto see,
And yee the swete savour fele,
You warrante may [I] right wele.
So thou thee kepe fro folye,
Shall no man do thee vylanye;
If I may helpe you in ought,
I shall not feyne, dredeth nought,
For I am bounde to youre servise,
Fully devoide of feyntise."
Thanne unto Bialacoil saide I:
"I thanke you, sir, full hertely
And youre biheeste take at gre,
That ye so goodly profer me.
To you it cometh of gret fraunchise
That ye me profer youre servise."
Thanne aftir, full delyverly,
Thorough the breres anoon wente I,
Wherof encombred was the hay.
I was wel plesed, the soth to say,
To se the bothon faire and swote
So freshe spronge out of the rote.
And Bialacoil me served well
Whanne I so nygh me myghte fele
Of the bothon the swete odour
And so lusty hewed of colour.
But thanne a cherle (foule hym bityde!)
Biside the roses gan hym hyde,
To kepe the roses of that roser
Of whom the name was DAUNGER.
This cherle was hid there in the greves,
Kovered with gras and with leves,
To spie and take whom that he fonde
Unto that Roser putte an honde.
He was not soole, for ther was moo;
For with hym were other twoo
Of wikkid maners and yvel fame.
That oon was clepid by his name
WYKKED-TONGE (god yeve hym sorwe!),
For neither at eve ne at morwe
He can of no man good [ne] speke;
On many a just man doth he wreke.
Ther was a womman eke that hight
SHAME, that, who can reken right,
Trespace was hir fadir name,
Hir moder Resoun; and thus was Shame
Brought of these ilke twoo.
And yitt hadde Trespasse never adoo
With Resoun, ne never ley hir bye
He was so hidous and so ugly,
I mene this that Trespas hight;
But resoun conceyved of a sight
Shame, of that I spake aforne.

nd whanne that Shame was thus [y-]
borne,
t was ordeyned that Chastite
hulde of the Roser lady be,
Vhich of the bothons more and lasse
Vith sondre folk assailed was,
'hat she ne wiste what to doo.
or Venus hir assailith soo,
'hat nyght and day from hir she stale
othons and roses over-all.
'o Resoun thanne praieth Chastite,
Vhom Venus hath flemed over the see,
'hat she hir doughter wolde hir lene,
'o kepe the Roser fresh and grene.
noon Resoun to Chastite
; fully assented that it be,
nd grauntide hir at hir request
'hat Shame, by cause she is honest,
hall keper of the roser be.
nd thus to kepe it ther were three,
'hat noon shulde hardy be ne bolde,
Vere he yong or were he olde,
geyn hir will awey to bere
othons ne roses that there were.
hadde wel spedde, hadde I not bene
wayted with these three and sene.
or Bialacoil, that was so faire,
o gracious and debonaire,
!uytt hym to me full curteislye,
nd me to please, bade that I
hulde drawe me to the bothon nere;
rese in to touche the rosere
Vhich bare the roses, he yaf me leve;
'his graunte ne myght but lytel greve.
nd for he sawe it liked me,
yght nygh the bothon pullede he
leef all grene and yaff me that;
'he whiche full nygh the bothon sat,
made [me] of that leef full queynte.

And whanne I felte I was aqueynte
With Bialacoil, and so pryve,
I wende all at my will hadde be.
Thanne waxe I hardy forto telle
To Bialacoil how me bifelle
Of love, that toke and wounded me;
And seide: "Sir, so mote I thee,
I may no joye have in no wise
Uppon no side, but it rise
For sithens, if I shall not feyne,
In herte I have hadde so gret peyne,
So gret annoy and such affray,
That I ne wote what I shall say,
I drede youre wrathe to disserve.
Lever me were that knyves kerve
My body shulde in pecys small,
Than any weyes it shulde fall
That ye wratthed shulde ben with me."
"Sey boldely thi will," quod he,
"I nyl be wroth, if that I may,
For nought that thou shalt to me say."
Thanne seide I, "Ser, not you displease
To knowen of myn gret unnese,
In which oonly love hath me brought.
For peynes gret, disese, and thought,
Fro day to day he doth me drye—
Supposeth not, sir, that I lye.
In me fyve woundes dide he make,
The soore of whiche shall nevere slake;
But ye the Bothon graunte me
Which is moost passaunt of beaute,
My lyf, my deth, and my martire,
And tresour, that I moost desire."
Thanne Bialacoil, affrayed all,
Seyde, "Sir, it may not fall—
That ye desire, it may not arise.
What! Wolde ye shende me in this
wise?
A mochel foole thanne I were,

If I suffride you awey to bere
The fresh bothoun so faire of sight.
For it were neither skile ne right,
Of the roser ye broke the rynde,
Or take the rose aforn his kynde;
Ye are not curteys to aske it.
Late it still on the roser sitt,
And growe til it amended be
And parfytly come to beaute;
I nolde not that it pulled were
Fro the roser that it bere,
To me it is so leef and deere."
With that sterte oute anoon Daungere,
Out of the place were he was hidde;
His malice in his chere was kidde.
Full grete he was and blak of hewe,
Sturdy and hidous, who so hym knewe,
Like sharp urchouns his here was growe;
His eyes reed as the fyre glowe,
His nose frounced, full kirked stoode.
He come criande as he were woode,
And seide: "Bialacoil, telle me why
Thou bryngest hider so booldely
Hym that [is] so nygh the roser!
Thou worchist in a wrong manner;
He thenkith to dishonoure thee.
Thou art wel worthy to have maugree,
To late hym of the roser wite;
Who serveth feloun is yvel quitte.
Thou woldist havė doon gret bounte,
And he with shame woulde quyte thee.
Fle hennes, Felowe! I rede thee goo,
It wanteth litel I wole thee sloo;
For Bialacoil ne knewe thee nought,
Whanne thee to serve he sette his
thought;
For thou wolt shame hym, if thou
myght,
Bothe ageyns resoun and right.
I wole no more in thee affye,
That comest so slyghly for tespye;
For it preveth wonder well
Thy sleight and tresoun every deell."
I durst no more there make abode
For the cherl, he was so wode;
So gan he threte and manace,
And thurgh the haye hedide me chace.
For feer of hym I tremblyde and quoke,
So cherlishly his heed it shoke;
And seide, if eft he myght me take
I shulde not from his hondis scape.
Thanne Bialacoil is fledde and mate,
And I, all soole, disconsolate,
Was left aloone in peyne and thought.
For shame to deth I was nygh brought.
Thanne thought I on myn high foly,
How that my body utterly
Was yeve to peyne and to martire;
And therto hadde I so gret ire,
That I ne durst the haye passe.
There was noon hope, there was no
grace,
I trowe nevere man wiste of peyne,
But he were laced in loves cheyne;
Ne no man [not], and sooth it is,
But if he love, what anger is.
Love holdith his heest to me right wele;
Whanne peyne he seide I shulde fele.
Noon herte may thenke, ne tunge seyne
A quarter of my woo and peyne;
I myght not with the anger laste.
Myn herte in poynt was forto brast,
Whanne I thought on the rose, that soo
Was thurgh Daunger cast me froo.
A longe while stode I in that state,
Til that me saugh so madde and mate
The lady of the highe ward,
Which from hir tour lokide thiderward

PEYNE

So gan he threte and manace,
And thurgh the haye he dide me chace
For feer of hym I tremblyde and quoke,
So cherlishly his heed it shoke;
And seide, if eft he myght me take
I shulde not from his hondis scape.
Thanne Bialacoil is fledde and mate,
And I, all soole, disconsolate,
Was left aloone in peyne and thought;
For shame to deth I was nygh brought.
Thanne thought I on myn high foly,
How that my body utterly
Was yeve to peyne and to martire;
And therto hadde I so gret ire,
That I ne durst the haye passe.
There was noon hope, there was no
grace,
I trowe nevere man wiste of peyne,
But he were laced in loves cheyne;
Ne no man [not], and sooth it is,
... what anger is.
... his heest to me right wel,
... he seide I shulde fele
... thenke, ne tunge seyn
... woo and peyne;
... the anger laste.
... was forto brast,
... on the rose, that so
... ger cast me froo.
... I in that state,
... so madde and mate
... he ward,
... lokide thiderward

Resoun men clepe that lady,
Which from hir tour delyverly,
Come doun to me withoute more.
But she was neither yong ne hoore,
Ne high ne lowe, ne fat ne lene,
But best as it were in a mene.
Hir eyen twoo were cleer and light
As ony candell that brenneth bright;
And in hir heed she hadde a crowne.
Hir semede wel an high persoune;
For rounde environ hir crownet
Was full of riche stonys frett.
Hir goodly semblaunt by devys
I trowe were maad in Paradys;
For nature hadde nevere such a grace
To forge a werk of such compace.
For certeyn, but if the letter lye,
God hym-silf, that is so high,
Made hir aftir his ymage,
And yaff hir sith sich avauntage,
That she hath myght and seignorie
To kepe men from all folye.
Who so wole trowe hir lore,
Ne may offenden nevermore.

And while I stode thus derk and pale,
Resoun bigan to me hir tale.
She seide: "Al hayle, my swete freende!
Foly and childhoode wole thee sheende,
Which the have putt in gret affray;
Thou hast bought deere the tyme of May,
That made thyn herte mery to be.
In yvell tyme thou wentist to see
The gardyne, wherof Idilnesse
Bare the keye and was maistresse,
Whanne thou yedest in the daunce
With hir, and haddest aqueyntaunce.
Hir aqueyntaunce is perilous,
First softe and aftir noious;
She hath [thee] trasshed withoute wene.
The God of Love hadde the not sene,
Ne hadde Idilnesse thee conveyed
In the verger, where Myrthe hym pleyed.
If foly have supprised thee,
Do so that it recovered be,
And be wel ware to take nomore,
Counsel that greveth aftir sore.
He is wise that wole hym-silf chastise;
And though a yong man in ony wise
Trespace amonge and do foly,
Late hym not tarye, but hastily
Late hym amende what so be mys.
And eke I counseile thee I-wys
The God of Love hoolly foryete,
That hath thee in sich peyne sette,
And thee in herte tourmented soo.
I can not sene how thou maist goo
Other weyes to garisoun;
For Daunger that is so feloun
Felly purposith thee to werreye,
Which is ful cruel, the soth to seye.

And yitt of Daunger cometh no blame
In rewarde of my doughter Shame,
Which hath the roses in her warde,
As she that may be no musarde.
And Wikked-Tunge is with these two,
That suffrith no man thider goo.
For er a thing be, do he shall,
Where that he cometh over-all,
In fourty places, if it be sought,
Seye thyng that nevere was don ne
wrought;
So moche tresoun is in his male,
Of falsnesse forto seyne a tale.
Thou delest with angry folk y-wis;
Wherfore to thee bettir is
From these folk awey to fare,

For they wole make thee lyve in care.
This is the yvell that love they calle,
Wherynne ther is but foly alle;
For love is foly everydell.
Who loveth in no wise may do well,
Ne sette his thought on no good werk.
His scole he lesith, if he be clerk;
Of other craft eke if he be,
He shal not thryve therynne, for he
In love shal have more passioun
Than monke, hermyte, or chanoun.
The peyne is hard out of mesure,
The joye may eke no while endure;
And in the possessioun,
Is mych tribulacioun.
The joye it is so short lastyng,
And but in happe is the getyng.
For I see there many in travaill
That atte laste foule fayle.
I was no thyng thi counseler
Whanne thou were maad the omager
Of God of Love to hastily.
Ther was no wisdom, but foly;
Thyne herte was joly but not sage,
Whanne thou were brought in sich a rage,
To yelde thee so redily.

And to leve of his gret maistrie,
I rede thee Love awey to dryve,
That makith thee recche not of thi lyve.
The foly more fro day to day
Shal growe, but thou it putte away.
Take with thy teeth the bridel faste
To daunte thyne herte, and eke thee
  caste,
If that thou maist gete thee defence,
Forto redresse thi first offence.
Who so his herte alwey wole leve
Shal fynde amonge that shal hym greve."

Whanne I hir herd thus me chastise,
I answerd in ful angry wise;
I prayed hir ceessen of hir speche,
Outher to chastise me or teche,
To bidde me my thought refreyne,
Which Love hath caught in his demeyne
"What! Wene ye Love wole consente,
That me assailith with bowe bente,
To drawe myne herte out of his honde,
Which is so qwikly in his bonde?
That ye counseyle may nevere be;
For whanne he firste arestide me,
He took myne herte so hoole hym tille,
That it is no thyng at my wille.
He taught it so hym forto obey,
That he it sparrede with a key.
I pray yow late me be all stille,
For ye may well, if that ye wille,
Youre wordis waste in idilnesse.
For utterly, withouten gesse,
All that ye seyn is but in veyne.
Me were lever dye in the peyne,
Than Love to-me-ward shulde arette
Falsheed, or tresoun on me sette.
I wole me gete prys or blame
And Love trewe to save my name;
Who that me chastith I hym hate."
With that word Resoun wente hir gate,
Whanne she saugh for no sermonynge
She myght me fro my foly brynge.
Thanne dismaied I, lefte all sool,
Forwery, forwandred, as a fool,
For I ne knewe no chevisaunce.
Thanne fell into my remembraunce
How Love bade me to purveye
A felowe, to whom I myght seye
My counsell and my pryvete,
For that shulde moche availe me.
With that bithought I me that I

THE LOVER LISTENING TO REASOUN

myte, or chanoun.
. out of mesure,
no while endure;
sioun,
oun.
hort lastyng,
is the getyng.
any in travaill
tle fayle.
i counseler
re maad the omager
o hastily.
om, but foly;
joly but not sage,
ebrought in sich arage,
edily.

gret maistrie,
awey to dryve,
recche not of thi lyve.
day to day
hou it putte away.
th the bridel faste
herte, and eke thee

gete thee defence,
first offence.
alwey wole leve

That ye counseyle may nevere be;
For whanne he firste arestide me,
He took myne herte so hoole hym tille
That it is no thyng at my wille.
He taught it so hym forto obey,
That he it sparrede with a key.
I pray yow late me be all stille,
For ye may well, if that ye wille,
Youre wordis waste in idilnesse.
For utterly, withouten gesse,
All that ye seyn is but in veyne.
Me were lever dye in the peyne,
Than Love to-me-ward shulde arette
Falsheed, or tresoun on me sette.
I wole me gete prys or blame
And Love trewe to save my name;
Who that me chastith I hym hate."
With that word Resoun wente hir gate,
Whanne she saugh for no sermonynge
She myght me fro my foly brynge.
Thanne dismaied I, lefte all sool,
Forwery, forwandred, as a fool,
For I ne knewe no chevisaunce.
Thanne fell into my remembraunce
How Love bad me to purveye
A felowe, to whom I myght seye
my pryvete,
moche availe me.
thoughte I me that I

Hadde a felowe faste by
Trewe and siker, curteys and hende;
And he was called by name a Freende,
A trewer felowe was no wher noon.
In haste to hym I wente anoon,
And to hym all my woo I tolde,
Fro hym right nought I wold witholde.
I tolde him all withoute were,
And made my compleynt on Daungere,
How forto see he was hidous,
And to-me-ward contrarious;
The whiche, thurgh his cruelte
Was in poynt to have meygned me.
With Bialacoil whanne he me sey
Withynne the gardeyn walke and pley,
Fro me he made hym forto go;
And I, bilefte aloone in woo,
I durst no lenger with hym speke,
For Daunger seide he wolde be wreke,
Whanne that he sawe how I wente
The freshe bothon forto hente,
If I were hardy to come neer
Bitwene the hay and the Roser.

This freend, whanne he wiste of my thought,
He discomforted me right nought,
But seide, "Felowe, be not so madde,
Ne so abaysshed, nor bystadde;
My silf I knowe full well Daungere,
And how he is feers of his cheere
At prime temps love to manace.
Ful ofte I have ben in his caas;
A feloun firste though that he be,
Aftir thou shalt hym souple se.
Of longe passed I knewe hym well;
Ungoodly first though men hym feele,
He wole meke aftir in his beryng
Been, for service and obeyssyng.
I shal thee telle what thou shalt doo:
Mekely I rede thou go hym to,
Of herte pray hym specialy
Of thy trespace to have mercy,
And hote well, [hym] here to plese,
That thou shalt nevermore hym displese.
Who can best serve of flaterie,
Shall please Daunger most uttirly."
My freend hath seid to me so wel,
That he me esid hath somdell,
And eke allegged of my torment.
For thurgh hym had I hardement
Agayn to Daunger forto go,
To preve if I myght meke hym soo.
To Daunger came I all ashamed,
The which aforn me hadde y-blamed,
Desiryng forto pese my woo.
But over hegge durst I not goo,
For he forbede me the passage.
I fonde hym cruel in his rage
And in his honde a gret burdoun.
To hym I knelide lowe a-doun,
Ful meke of port and symple of chere,
And seide, "Sir, I am comen heere
Oonly to aske of you mercy;
It greveth me full gretly
That evere my lyf I wratthed you.
But forto amenden I am come now,
With all my myght, bothe loude and stille,
To doon right at youre owne wille.
For Love made me forto doo
That I have trespassed hidirto,
Fro whom I ne may withdrawe myne herte.
Yit shall never for joy ne smerte,
What so bifalle, good or ille,
Offende more ageyn youre wille;
Lever I have endure disese,
Than do that you shulde displese.

I you require and pray that ye
Of me have mercy and pitee
To stynte your ire that greveth soo.
That I wole swere for ever mo
To be redressid at youre likyng,
If I trespasse in ony thyng.
Save that I pray thee graunte me
A thyng that may not warned be:
That I may love all oonly,
Noon other thyng of you aske I.
I shall doon elles well I-wys,
If of youre grace ye graunte me this;
And ye may not letten me,
For wel wot ye that love is free,
And I shall loven sithen that I wille,
Who evere like it, well or ille.
And yit ne wold I for all Fraunce
Do thyng to do you displesaunce."

Thanne Daunger fille in his entent
Forto foryeve his male talent;
But all his wratthe yit atte laste
He hath relesed, I preyde so faste.
Shortly he seide, "Thy request
Is not to mochel dishonest,
Ne I wole not werne it thee;
For yit no thyng engreveth me.
For though thou love thus evermore,
To me is neither softe ne soore.
Love where the list, what recchith me,
So [thou] fer fro my roses be?
Trust not on me for noon assay,
If ony tyme thou passe the hay."
Thus hath he graunted my praiere.
Thanne wente I forth withouten were
Unto my freend, and tolde hym all,
Which was right joyfull of my tale.
He seide, "Now goth wel thyn affaire,
He shall to thee be debonaire;
Though he aforn was dispitous,
He shall heere aftir be gracious.
If he were touchid on somme good
veyne,
He shuld yit rewen on thi peyne.
Suffre I rede, and no boost make,
Till thou at good mes maist hym take.
By sufferaunce and wordis softe
A man may overcome ofte
Hym that aforn he hadde in drede,
In bookis sothly as I rede."
Thus hath my freend with gret comfort
Avaunced me with high disport,
Which wolde me good as mych as I.
And thanne anoon full sodeynly
I toke my leve, and streight I wente
Unto the hay, for gret talent
I hadde to sene the fresh bothoun
Wherynne lay my salvacioun.
And Daunger toke kepe, if that I
Kepe hym covenaunt trewely.
So sore I dradde his manasyng
I durst not breke his biddyng,
For lest that I were of hym shent
I brake not his comaundement,
Forto purchase his good wille.
It was [nat] forto come ther-tille,
His mercy was to ferre bihynde;
I wepte for I ne myght it fynde.
I compleyned and sighed sore,
And langwisshed evermore,
For I durst not over goo
Unto the rose I loved soo.
Thurgh my demenyng outerly
[Thanne he had knowlege certanly,]
That Love me ladde in sich a wise
That in me ther was no feyntise,
Falsheed, ne no trecherie.
And yit he full of vylanye,

UNTO MY FREEND, AND TOLDE HYM ALL

thee graunte me
y not warned be :
all oonly,
g of you aske I.
well I-wys,
ye graunte me this ;
letten me,
hat love is free,
sithen that I wille,
t, well or ille.
I for all Fraunce
ou displesaunce."

fille in his entent
male talent ;
ne yit atte laste
I preyde so faste.
"Thy request
dishonest,
erne it thee ;
engreveth me.
love thus evermore,

Till thou at good mes maist hym take.
By sufferaunce and wordis softe
A man may overcome ofte
Hym that aforn he hadde in drede,
In bookis sothly as I rede."
Thus hath my freend with gret comfort
Avaunced me with high disport,
Which wolde me good as mych as I.
And thanne anoon full sodeynly
I toke my leve, and streight I wente
Unto the hay, for gret talent
I hadde to sene the fresh bothoun
Wherynne lay my salvacioun.
And Daunger toke kepe, if that I
Kepe hym covenaunt trewely.
So sore I dradde his manasyng
I durst not breke his biddyng,
For lest that I were of hym shent
I brake not his comaundement,
Forto purchase his good wille.
It was [nat] forto come ther-tille,
His mercy was to ferre bihynde ;
I wepte for I ne myght it fynde.
... and sighed sore,
... evermore,
... ever goo
... soo.
... outerly
... knowlege certanly,]
... in sich a wise
... no feyntise,
...erie.
... vylanye,

Of disdeyne, and cruelte,
On me ne wolde have pite
His cruel will forto refreyne,
Though I wepe alwey and me com-
pleyne.
And while I was in this torment,
Were come of grace, by god sent,
Fraunchise and with hir Pite.
Fulfild the bothen of bounte,
They go to Daunger anoon-right,
To forther me with all her myght,
And helpe in worde and in dede;
For well they saugh that it was nede.
First of hir grace dame Fraunchise
Hath taken [word] of this emprise;
She seide, "Daunger, gret wrong ye do
To worche this man so myche woo,
Or pynen hym so angerly;
It is to you gret villanye.
I can not see [ne] why ne how
That he hath trespassed ageyn you,
Save that he loveth; wherfore ye shulde
The more in cherete of hym holde.
The force of love makith hym do this;
Who wolde hym blame, he dide amys.
He leseth more than ye may do;
His peyne is harde, ye may see lo,
And Love in no wise wolde consente
That he have power to repente.
For though that quyk ye wolde hym sloo,
Fro love his herte may not goo.
Now, swete Sir, is it youre ese
Hym forto angre or disese?
Allas, what may it you avaunce
To done to hym so gret grevaunce?
What worship is it agayn hym take,
Or on youre man a werre make,
Sith he so lowly every wise
Is redy, as ye lust devise?
If Love hath caught hym in his lace
You for tobeye in every caas,
And ben youre suget at youre will,
Shuld ye therfore willen hym ill?
Ye shulde hym spare more all oute
Than hym that is bothe proude and
stoute.
Curtesie wole that ye socour
Hem that ben meke undir youre cure.
His herte is hard that wole not meke,
Whanne men of mekenesse hym biseke."
"That is certeyn," seide Pite,
"We se ofte that humilite
Bothe ire and also felonye
Venquyssheth, and also malencolye,
To stonde forth in such duresse,
This cruelte and wikkidnesse.
Wherfore I pray you, Sir Daungere,
Forto mayntene no lenger heere
Such cruel werre agayn youre man,
As hoolly youres as ever he can;
Nor that ye worchen no more woo
On this caytif that langwisshith soo,
Which wole no more to you trespasse,
But putte hym hoolly in youre grace.
His offense ne was but lite;
The god of Love it was to wite,
That he youre thrall so gretly is;
And if ye harme hym, ye done amys.
For he hath hadde full hard penaunce,
Sith that ye refte hym thaqueyntaunce
Of Bialacoil, his moste joye,
Which alle hise peynes myght acoye.
He was biforn anoyed sore,
But thanne ye doubled hem well more.
For he of blis hath ben full bare,
Sith Bialacoil was fro hym fare.
Love hath to hym do gret distresse,
He hath no nede of more duresse;

Voideth from hym youre ire, I rede,
Ye may not wynnen in this dede.
Makith Bialacoil repeire ageyn,
And haveth pite upon his peyne;
For Fraunchise wole and I, Pite,
That mercyful to hym ye be.
And sith that she and I accorde
Have upon hym misericorde,
For I you pray and eke moneste
Nought to refusen oure requeste.
For he is hard and fell of thought,
That for us twoo wole do right nought."

Daunger ne myght no more endure,
He mekede hym unto mesure.
"I wole in no wise," seith Daungere,
"Denye that ye have asked heere,
It were to gret uncurtesie;
I wole he have the companye
Of Bialacoil, as ye devise;
I wole hym lette in no wise."
To Bialacoil thanne wente in hye
Fraunchise, and seide full curteislye:
"Ye have to longe be deignous
Unto this lover and daungerous,
Fro hym to withdrawe your presence,
Whiche hath do to him great offence,
That ye not wolde upon him se;
Wherfore a sorouful man is he.
Shape ye to paye him, and to please,
Of my love if ye wol have ease;
Fulfyl his wyl, sithe that ye knowe
Daunger is daunted and brought lowe
Through helpe of me and of Pyte;
You dare no more aferde be."

"I shal do right as ye wyl."
Saith Bialacoil, "for it is skyl,
Sithe Daunger wol that it so be."
Than Fraunchise hath him sent to me
Bialacoil at the begynnyng,
Salued me in his commyng;
No straungenesse was in him sene,
No more than he ne had wrathed bene.
As fayre semblaunt than shewed he me,
And goodly, as aforne dyd he.
And by the honde withoute doute,
Within the haye right al aboute
He ladde me with right good chere,
Al envyron the vergere
That Daunger hadde me chased fro.
Nowe have I leave over al to go,
Nowe am I raysed at my devyse
Fro helle unto paradyse.
Thus Bialacoil of gentylnesse,
With al his payne and besynesse,
Hath shewed me onely of grace
The estres of the swote place.

I sawe the Rose whan I was nygh
Was greatter woxen and more high,
Fresshe, roddy, and fayre of hewe,
Of coloure veer yliche newe.
And whan I hadde it longe sene,
I sawe that through the leves grene
The Rose spredde to spaunysshinge,
To sene it was a goodly thynge.
But it ne was so sprede on brede
That men within myght knowe the sede
For it covert was and close
Bothe with the leves and with the rose.
The stalke was even and grene upright,
It was theron a goodly syght,
And wel the better, withoute wene,
For the seed was nat [y-]sene.
Ful fayre it spradde (God it blesse),
For suche another, as I gesse,
Aforne ne was, ne more vermayle.

I was abawed for marveyle,
For ever the fayrer that it was,
The more I am bounde in Loves laas.
Longe I abode there, sothe to saye,
Tyl Bialacoil I ganne to praye,
Whan that I sawe him, in no wyse
To me warnen his servyce,
That he me wolde graunt a thynge,
Whiche to remembre is wel syttynge.
This is to sayne, that of his grace
He wolde me yeve leysar and space,
To me that was so desyrous
To have a kyssynge precious
Of the goodly fresshe Rose,
That so swetely smelleth in my nose.
"For if it you displeased nought
I wolde gladly, as I have sought,
Have a cosse therof freely
Of your yefte; for certainly
I wol none have, but by your leve,
So lothe me were you for to greve."

He sayde, "Frende, so god me spede,
Of Chastite I have suche drede,
Thou shuldest nat warned be for me;
But I dare nat for Chastyte.
Agayne her dare I nat mysdo,
For alwaye byddeth she me so
To yeve no lover leave to kysse.
For who therto maye wynne y-wisse,
He of the surplus of the praye
May lyve in hoope to gette some daye.
For who so kyssynge maye attayne
Of loves payne hath, soth to sayne,
The best and [the] most avenaunt,
And ernest of the remenaunt."

Of his answere I sighed sore;
I durst assaye him tho no more,
I hadde suche drede to greve him aye.
A man shulde nat to moche assaye
To chafe hys frende out of measure,
Nor putte his lyfe in aventure.
For no man at the firste stroke
Ne maye nat felle downe an oke,
Nor of the reysyns have the wyne,
Tyl grapes be rype, and wel afyne
Be sore empressid, I you ensure,
And drawen out of the pressure.
But I forpeyned wonder stronge,
Though that I aboode right longe
Aftir the kis in peyne and woo,
Sith I to kis desired soo;
Till that, rewyng on my distresse,
Ther come Venus the goddesse,
Which ay werreyeth Chastite,
Came of hir grace to socoure me,
Whos myght is knowe ferre and wide;
For she is modir of Cupide,
The god of love, blynde as stoon,
That helpith lovers many oon.
This lady brought in hir right honde
Of brennyng fyre a blasyng bronde,
Wherof the flawme and hoote fire
Hath many a lady in desire
Of love brought, and sore hette,
And in hir servise her hertes sette.
This lady was of good entaile,
Right wondirfull of apparayle;
Bi hir atyre so bright and shene
Men myght perceyve well and sene
She was not of religioun.
Nor I nell make mencioun
Nor of robe nor of tresour,
Of broche nor of hir riche attour,
Ne of hir girdill aboute hir side,
For that I nyll not longe abide.
But knowith wel that certeynly

She was araied richely;
Devoyde of pruyde certeyn she was.
To Bialacoil she wente apas,
And to hym, shortly in a clause,
She seide, "Sir, what is the cause
Ye ben of port so daungerous
Unto this lover and deynous,
To graunte hym nothyng but a kisse.
To werne it hym ye done amysse,
Sith well ye wote how that he
Is loves servaunt, as ye may see,
And hath beaute, wher-through is
Worthy of love to have the blis.
How he is semely, biholde and see
How he is faire, how he is free,
How he is swoote and debonaire,
Of age yonge, lusty and faire.
Ther is no lady so hawteyne,
Duchesse ne countesse, ne chasteleyne,
That I nolde holde hir ungoodly
Forto refuse hym outterly.
His breth is also good and swete,
And eke his lippis rody, and mete
Oonly to pleyen and to kisse;
Graunte hym a kis of gentilnysse.
His teth arn also white and clene.
Methenkith [it] wrong, withouten wene,
If ye now werne hym, trustith me,
To graunte that a kis have he.
The lasse to helpe hym that ye haste,
The more tyme shul ye waste."
Whanne the flawme of the verry bronde,
That Venus brought in hir right honde,
Hadde Bialacoil with hete smete,
Anoon he bade me withouten lette,
Grauntede to me the Rose kisse.
Thanne of my peyne I gan to lysse,
And to the Rose anoon wente I,
And kisside it full feithfully.
Thar no man aske if I was blithe
Whanne the savour soft and lythe
Stroke to myn herte withoute more,
And me alegged of my sore,
So was I full of joye and blisse.
It is faire sich a flour to kisse;
It was so swoote and saverous.
I myght not be so angwisshous,
That I [ne] mote glad and joly be,
Whanne that I remembre me.
Yit ever among, sothly to seyne,
I suffre noye and moche peyne.
The see may never be so stille,
That with a litel wynde it nylle
Overwhelme and turne also,
As it were woode in wawis goo.
Aftir the calme, the trouble soone
Mote folowe, and chaunge as the moone.
Right so farith Love, that selde in oon
Holdith his anker: for right anoon,
Whanne they in ese wene beste to
lyve,
They ben with tempest all fordryve.
Who serveth love can telle of woo;
The stoundemele joie mote overgoo;
Now he hurteth and now he cureth,
For selde in oo poynt love endureth.

Now is it right me to procede
How Shame gan medle, and take hede,
Thurgh whom fele angres I have hadde,
And how the stronge wall was maad,
And the castell of brede and lengthe,
That God of Love wanne with his
strengthe.
All this in Romance will I sette,
And for no thyng ne will I lette,
So that it lykyng to hir be
That is the flour of beaute.

For she may best my labour quyte,
That I for hir love shal endite.

Wikkid-Tunge, that the covyne
Of every lover can devyne
Worste, and addith more somdell
(For wikkid tunge seith never well),
To-me-ward bare he right gret hate,
Espiyng me erly and late,
Till he hath sene the grete chere
Of Bialacoil and me I-feere.
He myghte not his tunge withstonde
Worse to reporte than he fonde,
He was so full of cursed rage;
It satte hym well of his lynage,
For hym an Irish womman bare.
His tunge was fyled sharpe and square,
Poign[i]aunt, and right kervyng,
And wonder bitter in spekyng.
For whanne that he me gan espie,
He swoore, affermyng sikirlye,
Bitwene Bialacoil and me
Was yvel aquayntaunce and pryve.
He spake therof so folilye,
That he awakide Ielousye,
Which all afrayed in his risyng,
Whanne that he herd [him] janglyng,
He ran anoon as he were woode
To Bialacoil there that he stode;
Which hadde lever in this caas
Have ben at Reynes or Amyas.
For foot-hoot in his felonye,
To hym thus seide Ielousie:
"Why hast thou ben so necligent
To kepen, whanne I was absent,
This verger heere left in thi warde.
To me thou haddist no rewarde,
To truste, to thy confusioun,
Hym thus, to whom suspeccioun
I have right gret, for it is nede;
It is well shewed by the dede.
Grete faute in thee now have I founde;
By God, anoon thou shalt be bounde,
And faste loken in a tour,
Withoute refuyt or socour.
For Shame to longe hath be thee froo;
Over soone she was agoo.
Whanne thou hast lost bothe drede and feere,
It semede wel she was not heere.
She was bisy in no wyse
To kepe thee and [to] chastise,
And forto helpen Chastite
To kepe the roser, as thenkith me.
For thanne this boy knave so booldely
Ne shulde not have be hardy,
[Ne] in this verger hadde such game,
Which now me turneth to gret shame."
Bialacoil nyst what to sey;
Full fayn he wolde have fled awey,
For feere han hidde, nere that he
All sodeynly toke hym with me.
And whanne I saugh he hadde soo,
This Ielousie, take us twoo,
I was a-stoned, and knewe no rede,
But fledde awey for verrey drede.
Thanne Shame cam forth full symplely.
She wende have trespaced full gretly,
Humble of hir port, and made it symple,
Weryng a vayle in stede of wymple,
As nonnys don in her abbey.
By cause hir herte was in affray,
She gan to speke withynne a throwe
To Ielousie right wonder lowe.
First of his grace she bysoughte
And seide, "Sire, ne leveth noughte
Wikkid-Tunge, that false espie,
Which is so glad to feyne and lye.

He hath you maad, thurgh flateryng,
On Bialacoil a fals lesyng;
His falsnesse is not now a-newe,
It is to long that he hym knewe;
This is not the firste day,
For Wikkid-Tunge hath custome ay
Yonge folkis to bewreye,
And false lesynges on hem leye.
Yit nevertheles I see amonge
That the loigne it is so longe
Of Bialacoil, hertis to lure
In Loves servyse forto endure,
Drawyng such folk hym too,
That he hath no thyng with to doo.
But in sothnesse I trowe nought
That Bialacoil hadde ever in thought
To do trespace or vylonye.
But for his modir Curtesie
Hath taught hym ever to be
Good of aqueyntaunce and pryve.
For he loveth noon hevynesse,
But mirthe, and pley, and all gladnesse;
He hateth all trechours,
Soleyn folk and envyou[r]s;
For ye witen how that he
Wole ever glad and joyfull be,
Honestly with folk to pleye.
I have be negligent in good feye
To chastise hym; therfore now I,
Of herte I crye you heere mercy
That I have been so recheles
To tamen hym, withouten lees.
Of my foly I me repente.
Now wole I hoole sette myn entente
To kepe, bothe low[d]e and stille,
Bialacoil to do youre wille."
"Shame, shame," seyde Ielousie,
"To be bytrasshed gret drede have I;
Leccherie hath clombe so hye,
That almoost blered is myn ye:
No wonder is if that drede have I;
Over all regnyth Lecchery,
Whos myght growith nyght and day
Bothe in cloistre and in abbey;
Chastite is werried over all,
Therfore I wole with siker wall
Close bothe roses and roser.
I have to longe in this maner
Left hem unclosid wilfully;
Wherfore I am right inwardly
Sorowfull, and repente me.
But now they shall no lenger be
Unclosid, and yit I drede sore
I shall repente ferthermore;
For the game goth all amys,
Counsell I must newe y-wys.
I have to longe tristed thee,
But now it shal no lenger be;
For he may best in every cost
Disceyve that men tristen most.
I see wel that I am nygh shent,
But if I sette my full entent
Remedye to purveye.
Therfore close I shall the weye,
Fro hem that wole the Rose espie,
And come to wayte me vilonye.
For in good feith and in trouthe,
I wole not lette for no slouthe,
To lyve the more in sikirnesse,
To make anoon a fort[e]resse,
Tenclose the roses of good savour.
In myddis shall I make a tour,
To putte Bialacoil in prisoun;
For evere I drede me of tresoun.
I trowe I shal hym kepe soo
That he shal have no myght to goo
Aboute, to make companye
To hem that thenke of vylanye;

Ne to no such as hath ben heere
Aforn, and founde in hym good chere;
Which han assailed hym to shende,
And with her trowandyse to blynde.
A foole is eythe to bigyle;
But, may I lyve a litel while,
He shal forthenke his fair semblaunt."

And with that word came DREDE avaunt,
Which was abasshed and in gret fere.
Whanne he wiste Ielousie was there,
He was for drede in sich affray,
That not a word durst he say,
But quakyng stode full still aloone,
Til Ielousie his weye was gone,
Save Shame, that him not forsoke.
Bothe Drede and she ful sore quoke,
Than atte laste Drede abreyde,
And to his cosyn Shame seide:
"Shame," he seide, "in sothfastnesse,
To me it is gret hevynesse
That the noyse so ferre is go,
And the sclaundre of us twoo;
But sithe that it is byfall,
We may it not ageyn call
Whanne onys sprongen is a fame.
For many a yeer withouten blame
We han ben, and many a day;
For many an Aprill and many a May
We han passed not [a-]shamed,
Till Ielousie hath us blamed
Of mystrust and suspecioun,
Causeles, withoute enchesoun.
Go we to Daunger hastily,
And late us shewe hym openly
That he hath not aright [y-]wrought,
Whanne that he sette nought his thought
To kepe better the purprise.
In his doyng he is not wise;
He hath to us do gret wronge,
That hath suffred now so longe
Bialacoil to have his wille,
All his lustes to fulfille.
He must amende it utterly,
Or ellys shall he vilaynesly
Exiled be out of this londe;
For he the werre may not withstonde
Of Ielousie, nor the greef,
Sith Bialacoil is at myscheef."
To Daunger, Shame and Drede anoon
The righte weye ben goon.
The cherle thei founden hem aforn
Liggyng undir an hawethorn;
Undir his heed no pilowe was,
But in the stede a trusse of gras.
He slombred, and a nappe he toke,
Tyll Shame pitously hym shoke,
And grete manace on hym gan make.
"Why slepist thou, whanne thou
shulde wake?"
Quod Shame. "Thou doist us
vylanye;
Who tristith thee, he doth folye,
To kepe roses or bothouns
Whanne thei ben faire in her sesouns.
Thou art woxe to familiere,
Where thou shulde be straunge of
chere,
Stoute of thi porte, redy to greve.
Thou doist gret folye forto leve
Bialacoil here inne to calle
The yonder man, to shende us alle.
Though that thou slepe, we may here
Of Ielousie gret noyse heere.
Art thou now late? Rise up an high,
And stoppe sone, and delyverly,
All the gappis of the hay;
Do no favour, I thee pray.

It fallith no thyng to thy name
To make faire semblaunt, where thou
maist blame.
Yf Bialacoil be sweete and free,
Dogged and fell thou shuldist be,
Froward and outerageous y-wis.
A cherl chaungeth that curteis is.
This have I herd ofte in seiyng,
"That man may, for no dauntyng,
Make a sperhauke of a bosarde."
Alle men wole holde thee for musarde
That debonair have founden thee.
It sittith thee nought curteis to be,
To do men plesaunce or servise;
In thee it is recreaundise.
Lete thi werkis fer and nere
Be like thi name, which is Daungere."

Thanne, all abawid in shewing,
Anoon spake Drede right thus seiyng,
And seide, "Daungere, I drede me
That thou ne wolt bisy be
To kepe that thou hast to kepe;
Whanne thou shuldist wake thou art
a slepe.
Thou shalt be greved certeynly,
If the aspie Ielousie,
Or if he fynde thee to blame.
He hath to day assailed Shame
And chased awey, with gret manace,
Bialacoil oute of this place,
And swereth shortly that he shall
Enclose hym in a sturdy wall;
And all is for thi wikkidnesse,
For that thee faileth straungenesse.
Thyne herte I trowe be failed all.
Thou shalt repente in speciall,
If Ielousie the sooth knewe;
Thou shalt forthenke and sore rewe."

With that the cherl his clubbe gan
shake,
Frounyng his eyen gan to make,
And hidous chere; as man in rage
For ire he brente in his visage.
Whanne that [he] herd hym blamed soo,
He seide, "Oute of my witte I goo;
To be discomfyt I have gret wronge.
Certis I have now lyved to longe,
Sith I may not this roser kepe.
All quykke I wolde be dolven deepe
If ony man shal more repeire
Into this gardyne, for foule or faire.
Myne herte for ire goth a-fere
That I lete ony entre heere.
I have do folie, now I see;
But now it shall amended bee.
Who settith foot heere ony more,
Truly he shall repente it sore,
For no man moo into this place
Of me to entre shal have grace.
Lever I hadde with swerdis tweyne
Thurghoute myne herte in every veyne
Perced to be with many a wounde,
Thanne slouthe shulde in me be founde.
From hennes forth, by nyght or day,
I shall defende it, if I may,
Withouten ony excepcioun
Of ech maner condicioun.
And if I it eny man graunte,
Holdeth me for recreaunte."

Thanne Daunger on his feet gan stonde,
And hente a burdoun in his honde.
Wroth in his ire, ne lefte he nought
But thurgh the verger he hath sought;
If he myght fynde hole or trace,
Where-thurgh that me mote forth by
pace,

Or ony gappe, he dide it close,
That no man myghte touche a rose.
Of the roser all aboute
He shitteth every man withoute.
Thus day by day Daunger is wers,
More wondirfull, and more dyvers,
And feller eke than evere he was.
For hym full ofte I synge "allas,"
For I ne may nought, thurgh his ire,
Recovere that I moost desire.
Myne herte, allas, wole brest a-twoo,
For Bialacoil I wratthed soo;
For certeynly in every membre
I quake whanne I me remembre
Of the bothon which I wolde
Full ofte a day sene and biholde.
And whanne I thenke upon the kisse,
And how mych joye and blisse
I hadde thurgh the savour swete,
For wante of it I grone and grete.
Me thenkith I fele yit in my nose
The swete savour of the rose.
And now I woot that I mote goo
So fer the freshe floures froo,
To me full welcome were the deth.
Absens therof allas me sleeth.
For whilom with this Rose, allas,
I touched nose, mouth, and face;
But now the deth I must abide.
But love consente another tyde
That onys I touche may and kisse,
I trowe my peyne shall never lisse.
Theron is all my coveitise,
Which brent myn herte in many wise.
Now shal repaire agayn sighinge,
Long wacche on nyghtis, and no slepinge,
Thought in wisshing, torment and woo,
With many a turnyng to and froo.
That half my peyne I can not telle,
For I am fallen into helle
From paradys, and wel the more
My turment greveth more and more.
Anoieth now the bittirnesse,
That I to forn have felt swetnesse.
And Wikkid-Tunge thurgh his falshede
Causeth all my woo and drede.
On me he leieth a pitous charge,
Bi-cause his tunge was to large.

Now it is tyme shortly that I
Telle you som-thyng of Ielousie,
That was in gret suspecioun.
Aboute hym lefte he no masoun,
That stoon coude leye, ne querrour;
He hirede hem to make a tour.
And first, the roses forto kepe,
Aboute hem made he a diche deepe,
Right wondir large, and also broode.
Upon the whiche also stode
Of squared stoon a sturdy wall,
Which on a cragge was founded all.
And right grete thikkenesse eke it bare
Abouten it was founded square,
An hundred fademe on every side.
It was aliche longe and wide;
Lest ony tyme it were assayled,
Ful wel aboute it was batayled,
And rounde enviroun eke were sette
Ful many a riche and faire tourette.
At every corner of this wall
Was sette a tour full pryncipall,
And everich hadde, withoute fable,
A porte-colys defensable
To kepe of enemyes, and to greve
That there her force wolde preve.
And eke amydde this purprise
Was maad a tour of gret maistrise;
A fairer saugh no man with sight,

Large, and wide, and of gret myght.
They dredde noon assaut
Of gynne, gunne, nor skaffaut.
The temprure of the mortere
Was maad of lycour wonder dere,
Of quykke lyme, persant and egre,
The which was tempred with vynegre.
The stoon was hard of ademant,
Wherof they made the foundement.
The tour was rounde, maad in compas;
In all this world no riccher was,
Ne better ordeigned therwith-all.
Aboute the tour was maad a wall,
So that bitwixt that and the tour
Rosers were sette of swete savour
With many roses that thei bere.
And eke withynne the castell were
Spryngoldes, gunnes, bows and archers,
And eke aboven atte corners
Men seyn over the walle stonde
Grete engynes, who were nygh honde.
And in the kernels heere and there
Of Arblasters grete plente were;
Noon armure myght her stroke with-
stonde,
It were foly to prece to honde.
Withoute the diche were lystes maade
With wall batayled large and brade,
For men and hors shulde not atteyne
To neighe the dyche over the pleyne.
Thus Ielousie hath enviroun
Sette aboute his garnysoun,
With walles rounde and diche depe,
Oonly the roser forto kepe.
And Daunger bere erly and late
The keyes of the utter gate,
The whiche openeth toward the eest.
And he hadde with hym atte leest
Thritty servauntes, echon by name.
That other gate kepte Shame,
Which openede, as it was couth,
Toward the part[i]e of the south.
Sergeauntes assigned were hir too
Ful many, hir wille forto doo.
Thanne Drede hadde in hir baillie
The kepyng of the Conestablerye,
Toward the north I undirstonde,
That openyde upon the lyfte honde.
The which for no thyng may be sure
But if she do bisy cure,
Erly on morowe and also late,
Strongly to shette and barre the gate.
Of every thing that she may see
Drede is aferd, wher so she be;
For with a puff of litell wynde
Drede is a-stonyed in hir mynde.
Therfore for stelyng of the Rose
I rede hir nought the yate unclose;
A foulis flight wole make hir flee,
And eke a shadowe if she it see.

Thanne Wikked-Tunge, full of envye,
With soudiours of Normandye,
As he that causeth all the bate,
Was keper of the fourthe gate.
And also to the tother three
He wente full ofte forto see.
Whanne his lotte was to wake anyght,
His instrumentis wolde he dight
Forto blowe and make sowne
(Ofte thanne he hath enchesoun)
And walken oft upon the wall,
Corners and wikettis over all
Full narwe serchen and espie.
Though he nought fonde, yit wole he lye
Discordaunt ever fro armonye,
And distoned from melodie.
Controve he wolde, and foule fayle

With hornepipes of Cornewaile;
In floytes made he discordaunce.
And in his musyk with myschaunce,
He wolde seyn with notes newe
That he fonde no womman trewe,
Ne that he saugh never in his lyf
Unto hir husbonde a trewe wyf;
Ne noon so ful of honeste,
That she nyl laughe and mery be
Whanne that she hereth, or may espie,
A man speken of leccherie.
Everiche of hem hath somme vice;
Oon is dishonest, another is nyce;
If oon be full of vylanye,
Another hath a likerous ighe;
If oon be full of wantonesse,
Another is a chideresse.

Thus Wikked Tunge (god yeve hem shame)
Can putt hem everychone in blame
Withoute desert, and causeles.
He lieth, though they ben giltles.
I have pite to sene the sorwe
That waketh bothe eve and morwe,
To Innocentis doith such grevaunce.
I pray god yeve hym evel chaunce,
That he ever so bisie is
Of ony womman to seyn amys.
Eke Ielousie God confounde,
That hath maad a tour so rounde,
And made aboute a garisoun
To sette Bealacoil in prisoun,
The which is shette there in the tour
Ful longe to holde there sojour,
There forto lyven in penaunce.
And forto do hym more grevaunce
Ther hath ordeyned Ielousie
An olde vekke forto espye
The maner of his governaunce.
The whiche devel in hir enfaunce
Hadde lerned of loves arte,
And of his pleyes toke hir parte.
She was expert in his servise,
She knewe eche wrenche and every gise
Of love, and every wile;
It was [the] harder hir to gile.
Of Bealacoil she toke ay hede,
That evere he lyveth in woo and drede.
He kepte hym koy and eye pryve,
Lest in hym she hadde see
Ony foly countenaunce;
For she knewe all the olde daunce.
And aftir this, whanne Ielousie
Hadde Bealacoil in his baillie,
And shette hym up that was so fre;
For seure of hym he wolde be.
He trusteth sore in his castell,
The stronge werk hym liketh well.
He dradde not that no glotouns
Shulde stele his roses or bothouns.
The roses weren assured all,
Defenced with the stronge wall.
Now Ielousie full well may be
Of drede devoide in liberte,
Whether that he slepe or wake,
For his roses may noon be take.

But I allas now morne shall
Bi-cause I was withoute the wall.
Full moche doole and moone I made.
Who hadde wist what woo I hadde,
I trowe he wolde have had pite.
Love to deere hadde soolde to me
The good, that of his love hadde I.
I wente a bought it all queyntly,
But now, thurgh doublyng of my peyne,
I see he wolde it selle ageyne,

And me a newe bargeyn leere,
The which all-oute the more is deere;
For the solace that I have lorn,
Thanne I hadde it never aforn.
Certayn I am ful like in deede
To hym that caste in erthe his seede,
And hath joie of the newe spryng,
Whanne it greneth in the gynnyng,
And is also faire and fresh of flour,
Lusty to seen, swoote of odour,
But er he it in sheves shere,
May falle a weder that shal it dere,
And maken it to fade and falle,
The stalke, the greyne, and floures alle,
That to the tylyer is fordone
The hope that he hadde to soone.
I drede certeyn that so fare I;
For hope and travaile sikerlye
Ben me byraft all with a storme;
The floure nel seeden of my corne.
For Love hath so avaunced me
Whanne I bigan my pryvite
To Bialacoil all forto telle,
Whom I ne fonde froward ne felle,
But toke a gree all hool my play.
But Love is of so hard assay,
That all at oonys he reved me,
Whanne I wente best aboven have be.
It is of love as of fortune,
That chaungeth ofte, and nyl contune;
Which whilom wole on folkes smyle,
And glowmbe on hem another while;
Now freend, now foo, shaltow hir feele.
For [in] a twynklyng, turne hir wheele,
She can writhe hir heed awey;
This is the concours of hir pley.
She canne arise that doth morne,
And whirle adown, and over turne.
Who sittith hieghst, but as hir lust?
A foole is he that wole hir trust.
For it is I that am come down
Thurgh change and revolucioun.
Sith Bealacoil mote fro me twynne,
Shette in the prisoun yonde withynne,
His absence at myn herte I fele.
For all my joye and all myne hele
Was in hym and in the rose,
That but yon walle, which hym doth close
Opene that I may hym see,
Love nyl not that I cured be
Of the peynes that I endure,
Nor of my cruel aventure.
A, Bialacoil, myn owne deere,
Though thou be now a prisonere,
Kepe atte leste thyne herte to me,
And suffre not that it daunted be;
Ne late not Ielousie in his rage
Putten thine herte in no servage.
Al though he chastice thee withoute,
And make thy body unto hym loute,
Have herte as hard as dyamaunt,
Stedefast, and nought pliaunt;
In prisoun though thi body be,
At large kepe thyne herte free.
A trewe herte wole not plie,
For no manace that it may drye.
If Ielousie doth thee payne,
Quyte hym his while thus agayne
To venge thee atte leest in thought,
If other way thou mai[e]st nought;
And in this wise sotilly
Worche and wynne the maistrie.
But yit I am in gret affray
Lest thou do not as I say;
I drede thou canst me gret maugre
That thou enprisoned art for me.
But that [is] not for my trespas,
For thurgh me never discovred was

"A, BIALACOIL, MYN OWNE DEERE"

rthe his seede,
ewe spryng,
the gynnyng,
esh of flour,
of odour,
here,
shal it dere,
and falle,
, and floures alle,
rdone
le to soone.
fare I;
sikerlye
a storme;
of my corne.
nced me
ryvite
elle,
vard ne felle,
l my play.
assay,
ved me,
aboven have be.
ne,
nd nyl contune;
n folkes smyle,
another while;
baltow hir feele.
urne hir wheele,
d awey;
hir pley.
oth morne,
[illegible]
ut as hir lust?

His absence at myn herte I fele.
For all my joye and all myne hele
Was in hym and in the rose,
That but yon walle, which hym doth clo[se]
Opene that I may hym see,
Love nyl not that I cured be
Of the peynes that I endure,
Nor of my cruel aventure.
A, Bialacoil, myn owne deere,
Though thou be now a prisonere,
Kepe atte leste thyne herte to me,
And suffre not that it daunted be;
Ne late not Ielousie in his rage
Putten thine herte in no servage.
Al though he chastice thee withoute,
And make thy body unto hym loute,
Have herte as hard as dyamaunt,
Stedefast, and nought pliaunt;
In prisoun though thi body be,
At large kepe thyne herte free.
A trewe herte wole not plie,
For no manace that it may drye.
If Ielousie doth thee payne,
Quyte hym his while thus agayne
To venge thee atte leest in thought,
If other way thou mai[e]st nought;
And in this wise sotilly
Worche and wynne the maistrie.
But yit I am in gret affray
Lest thou do not as I say;
I drede thou canst me gret maugre
That thou enprisoned art for me.
[illegible] for my trespas,
For thurgh me never discovred was

That thyng that oughte be secree.
Wel more anoye is in me
Than is in thee of this myschaunce,
For I endure more harde penaunce
Than ony [man] can seyn or thynke;
That for the sorwe almost I synke.
Whanne I remembre me of my woo,
Full nygh out of my witt I goo
Inward myn herte I feele blede;
For comfortles the deth I drede.
Owe I not wel to have distresse
Whanne false thurgh hir wikkednesse
And traitours, that arn envyous,
To noyen me be so curious?
A, Bialacoil, full wel I see
That they hem shape to disceyve thee,
To make thee buxom to her lawe,
And with her corde thee to drawe
Where so hem lust, right at her wille;
I drede they have thee brought thertille.
Withoute comfort thought me sleeth,
This game wole brynge me to my deeth;
For if youre good[e] wille I leese,
I mote be deed, I may not chese;
And if that thou foryete me,
Myne herte shal nevere in likyng be,
Nor elles where fynde solace,
If I be putt out of youre grace,
As it shal never been, I hope.
Thanne shulde I fallen in wanhope.
Allas—in wanhope? nay pardee,
For I wole never dispeired be.
If hope me faile, thanne am I
Ungracious and unworthy.
In hope I wole comforted be,
For Love, whanne he bitaught hir me,
Seide that Hope, where so I goo,
Shulde ay be reles to my woo.
But what and she my baalis beete,
And be to me curteis and sweete?
She is in no thyng full certeyne.
Lovers she putt in full gret peyne,
And makith hem with woo to deele;
Hir faire biheeste disceyveth feele.
For she wole byhote sikirly,
And failen aftir outrely.
A, that is a full noyous thyng!
For many a lover in lovyng
Hangeth upon hir, and trusteth fast,
Whiche leese her travel at the last.
Of thyng to comen she woot right nought;
Therfore if it be wysely sought,
Hir counseill foly is to take.
For many tymes whanne she wole make
A full good silogisme, I dreede
That aftirward ther shal in deede
Folwe an evell conclusioun.
This putte me in confusioun;
For many tymes I have it seen
That many have bigyled been
For trust that they have sette in hope,
Which felle hem aftirward a-slope.
But nevertheles yit gladly she wolde
That he, that wole hym with hir holde,
Hadde alle tymes his purpos clere,
Withoute deceyte or ony were;
That she desireth sikirly.
Whanne I hir blamed, I dide foly.
But what avayleth hir good wille?
Whanne she ne may staunche my
  stounde ille,
That helpith litel that she may doo,
Outake biheest unto my woo.
And heeste certeyn, in no wise
Withoute yift is not to prise.
Whanne heest and deede a-sundry varie,
They doon a gret contrarie.
Thus am I possed up and doun

With dool, thought, and confusioun;
Of my disese ther is no noumbre.
Daunger and Shame me encumbre,
Drede also, and Ielousie,
And Wikked-Tunge full of envie,
Of whiche the sharpe and cruel ire
Full ofte me putte in gret martire.
They han my joye fully lette,
Sith Bialacoil they have bishette
Fro me in prisoun wikkidly,
Whom I love so entierly
That it wole my bane bee
But I the sonner may hym see.
And yit more over, wurst of all,
Ther is sette to kepe (foule hir bifall!)
A rympled vekke, ferre ronne in age,
Frownyng and yelowe in hir visage,
Which in a-wayte lyth day and nyght,
That noon of hym may have a sight.
Now mote my sorwe enforced be;
Full soth it is that Love yaf me
Three wonder yiftes, of his grace,
Whiche I have lorn now in this place,
Sith they ne may, withoute drede,
Helpen but lytel, who taketh heede.
For here availeth no Swete-Thought,
And Sweete-Speche helpith right
nought;
The thridde was called Swete-Lokyng,
That now is lorn without lesyng.
Yiftes were faire, but not forthy
They helpe me but symplely
But Bialacoil loosed be,
To gon at large and to be free.
For hym my lyf lyth all in doute,
But if he come the rather oute.
Allas, I trowe it wole not bene!
For how shult I evermore hym sene?
He may not oute, and that is wronge,
By cause the tour is so stronge.
How shulde he oute? By whos prowesse,
Oute of so stronge a forteresse?
By me certeyn it nyl be doo;
God woot I have no witte therto.
But wel I woot I was in rage,
Whonne I to Love dide homage.
Who was the cause, in sothfastnesse,
But hir-silf Dame Idelnesse,
Which me conveied, thurgh my praiere,
To entre into that faire verger?
She was to blame me to leve,
The which now doth me soore greve.
A foolis word is nought to trowe,
Ne worth an appel forto love.
Men shulde hym snybbe bittirly
At pryme temps of his foly.
I was a fool and she me leevede,
Thurgh whom I am right nought
releeved;
She accomplisshid all my wille,
That now me greveth wondir ille.
Resoun me seide what shulde falle.
A fool my silf I may wel calle
That love asyde I hadde not leyde,
And trowed that dame Resoun seide.
Resoun hadde bothe skile and ryght,
Whanne she me blamed with all hir
myght
To medle of love that hath me shent;
But certyn now I wole repente.

And shulde I repente? Nay, parde,
A fals traitour thanne shulde I be.
The develes engynnes wolde me take,
If I my lorde wolde forsake,
Or Bialacoil falsly bitraye.
Shulde I at myscheef hate hym? Nay,
Sith he now for his curtesie

Is in prisoun of Ielousie.
Curtesie certeyn dide he me,
So mych that may not yolden be,
Whanne he the hay passen me lete
To kisse the Rose faire and swete;
Shulde I therfore cunne hym mawgre?
Nay, certeynly, it shal not be;
For Love shall nevere, yif God wille,
Here of me, thurgh word or wille,
Offence or complaynt more or lesse,
Neither of Hope nor Idilnesse.
For certis it were wrong that I
Hated hem for her curtesie.
Ther is not ellys but suffre and thynke,
And waken whanne I shulde wynke;
Abide in hope til Love, thurgh chaunce,
Sende me socour or allegeaunce,
Expectant ay till I may mete
To geten mercy of that swete.

Whilom I thenke how love to me
Seide he wolde take att gree
My servise, if unpacience
Caused me to done offence.
He seide, "In thank I shal it take,
And high maister eke thee make,
If wikkednesse ne reve it thee;
But, sone, I trowe that shall not be."
These were his wordis by and by;
It semede he lovede me trewely.
Now is ther not but serve hym wele,
If that I thenke his thanke to fele;
My good, myne harme lyth hool in me.
In love may no defaute be,
For trewe Love ne failide never man;
Sothly the faute mote nedys than,
As god forbede, be founde in me.
And how it cometh, I can not see;
Now late it goon as it may goo,
Whether Love wole socoure me or sloo;
He may do hool on me his wille;
I am so sore bounde hym tille,
From his servise I may not fleen;
For lyf and deth, withouten wene,
Is in his hande, I may not chese,
He may me doo bothe wynne and leese.
And sith so sore he doth me greve,
Yit if my lust he wolde acheve
To Bialacoil goodly to be,
I yeve no force what felle on me.
For though I dye as I mote nede,
I praye Love of his goodlyhede
To Bialacoil do gentylnesse,
For whom I lyve in such distresse,
That I mote deyen for penaunce.
But first withoute repentaunce,
I wole me confesse in good entent,
And make in haste my testament,
As lovers doon that feelen smerte.
To Bialacoil leve I myne herte
All hool withoute departyng,
Or doublenesse of repentyng.

Thus as I made my passage
In compleynt, and in cruel rage,
And I not where to fynde a leche
That couthe unto myne helpyng eche,
Sodeynly agayn comen doun
Out of hir tour I saugh Resoun,
Discrete, and wis, and full plesaunt,
And of hir porte full avenaunt.
The righte weye she tooke to me,
Which stode in gret perplexite,
That was posshed in every side,
That I nyst where I myght abide;
Till she demurely sad of chere,
Seide to me, as she come nere,
"Myne owne freend, art thou yit greved?

How is this quarell yit acheved
Of Loves side? Anoon me telle.
Hast thou not yit of Love thi fille?
Art thou not wery of thy servise
That the hath in siche wise?
What joye hast thou in thy lovyng?
Is it swete or bitter thyng?
Canst thou yit chese, late me see,
What best thi socour myght be?
Thou servest a full noble lorde,
That maketh thee thrall for thi rewarde,
Which ay renewith thi turment,
With foly so he hath thee blent.
Thou fell in mycheef thilke day
Whanne thou didist, the sothe to say,
Obeysaunce and eke homage.
Thou wroughtest no-thyng as the sage,
Whanne thou bicam his liege man;
Thou didist a gret foly than,
Thou wistest not what fell therto,
With what lord thou haddist to do;
If thou haddist hym wel knowe,
Thou haddist nought be brought so lowe.
For if thou wistest what it were,
Thou noldist serve hym half a yeer,
Not a weke nor half a day,
Ne yit an hour withoute delay,
Ne never ha lovede paramours.
His lordshipp is so full of shoures,
Knowest hym ought?"
L'Amaunt. "Ye, Dame, parde.
Raisoun. "Nay, nay."
L'Amaunt. "Yis, I."
Raisoun. "Wherof? late se."
L'Amaunt. "Of that he seide I shulde be
Glad to have sich lord as he,
And maister of sich seignorie."
Raisoun. "Knowist hym no more?"
L'Amaunt. "Nay, certis, I,
Save that he yaf me rewles there,
And wente his wey, I nyste where,
And I aboode bounde in balaunce."
Raisoun. "Lo, there a noble conisaunce!
But I wille that thou knowe hym now,
Gynnyng and eende, sith that thou
Art so anguisshous and mate,
Disfigured oute of a-state;
Ther may no wrecche have more of woo,
Ne caytyfe noon enduren soo.
It were to every man sittyng
Of his lord have knowleching;
For if thou knewe hym oute of doute,
Lightly thou shulde escapen oute
Of the prisoun that marreth thee."
L'Amaunt. "Ye, Dame, sith my lord is he,
And I his man maad with myn honde,
I wolde right fayne undirstonde
To knowen of what kynde he be,
If ony wolde enforme me."
Raisoun. "I wolde," seide Resoun, "thee lere
Sith thou to lerne hast sich desire,
And shewe thee withouten fable,
A thyng that is not demonstrable.
Thou shalt [wite] withouten science,
And knowe withouten experience,
The thyng that may not knowen be,
Ne wist ne shewid in no degre.
Thou maist the sothe of it not witen,
Though in thee it were writen.
Thou shalt not knowe therof more,
While thou art reuled by his lore.
But unto hym that love wole flee
The knotte may unclosed bee,

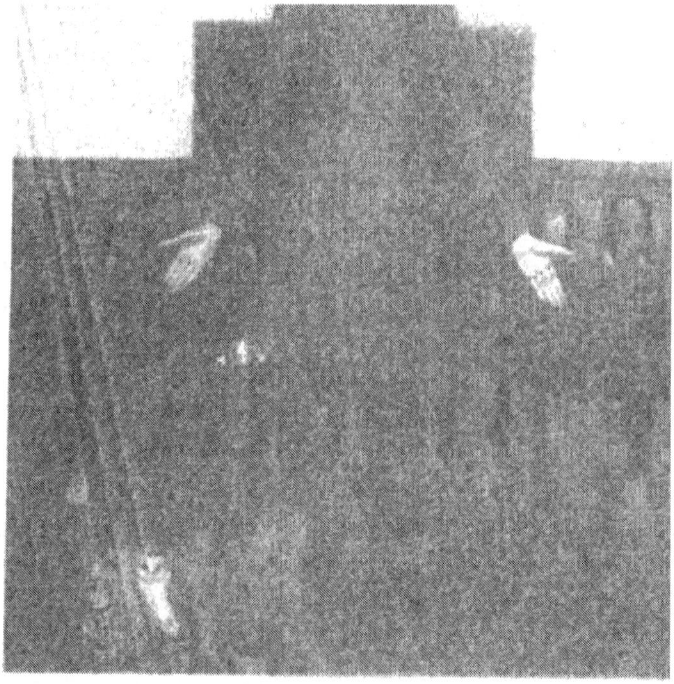

SWEET REASON

It were to every man sittyng
Of his lord have knowleching;
For if thou knewe hym oute of doute,
Lightly thou shulde escapen oute
Of the prisoun that marreth thee."
L'Amaunt. "Ye, Dame, sith my lord is he,
And I his man maad with myn honde
I wolde right fayne undirstonde
To knowen of what kynde he be,
If ony wolde enforme me."
Raisoun. "I wolde," seide Resoun, "thee lere
Sith thou to lerne hast sich desire,
And shewe thee withouten fable,
A thyng that is not demonstrable.
Thou shalt [wite] withouten science,
And knowe withouten experience,
The thyng that may not knowen be,
Ne wist ne shewid in no degre.
Thou maist the sothe of it not witen,
Though in thee it were writen.
Thou shalt not knowe therof more,
While thou art reuled by his lore.
But unto hym that love wole flee
The knotte may unclosed bee,

Which hath to thee, as it is founde,
So long be knette and not unbounde.
Now sette wel thyne entencioun,
To here of love discripcioun.

Love it is an hatefull pees,
A free acquitaunce withoute relees,
A truthe frette full of falsheede;
A sikernesse all sette in drede,
In hertis a dispeiryng hope,
And full of hope it is wanhope;
Wise woodnesse and wode resoun,
A swete perell in to droune,
An hevy birthen lyght to bere;
A wikked wawe alwey to ware,
It is Karibdous perilous;
Disagreable and gracious;
It is discordaunce that can accorde,
And accordaunce to discorde;
It is kunnyng withoute science,
Wisdome withoute sapience,
Witte withoute discrecioun,
Havoire withoute possessioun;
It is sike hele and hool sekenesse,
A thrust drowned in dronknesse;
An helthe full of maladie,
And charite full of envie;
An hunger full of habundaunce,
And a gredy suffisaunce;
Delite right ful of hevynesse,
And drerihed full of gladnesse;
Bitter swetnesse and swete errour,
Right evell savoured good savour;
Syn[ne] that pardoun hath withynne,
And pardoun spotted oute with synne;
A peyne also it is joious,
And felonye right pitous;
Also pley that selde is stable,
And stedefast [stat] right mevable.
A strengthe weyked to stonde upright,
And feblenesse full of myght;
Witte unavised, sage folie,
And joie full of turmentrie;
A laughter it is, weping ay,
Reste that traveyleth nyght and day;
Also a swete helle it is,
And a soroufull paradys;
A plesaunt gayl and esy prisoun,
And, full of froste, [a] somer sesoun,
Pryme temps full of frostes white,
And May devoide of al delite;
With seer braunches blossoms ungrene,
And newe fruyt fillid with wynter tene.
It is a slowe may not forbere
Ragges ribaned with gold to were;
For also well wole love be sette
Under ragges as riche rochette,
And eke as wel by amourettes
In mournyng blak, as bright burnettes.
For noon is of so mochel pris,
Ne no man founden [is] so wys,
Ne noon so high is of parage,
Ne no man founde of witt so sage,
No man so hardy, ne so wight,
Ne no man of so mychel myght,
Noon so fulfilled of bounte,
That he with love [ne] may daunted be.
All the world holdith this wey,
Love makith all to goon myswey,
But it be they of yvel lyf
Whom Genius cursith man and wyf,
That wrongly werke ageyn nature.
Noon such I love, ne have no cure
Of sich as loves servauntes bene,
And wole not by my counsel flene.
For I ne preise that lovyng,
Wherthurgh men at the laste eendyng
Shall calle hem wrecchis full of woo,

Love greveth hem and shendith soo.
But if thou wolt wel love eschewe
Forto escape out of his mewe,
And make al hool thi sorwe to slake,
No bettir counsel maist thou take
Than thynke to fleen wel I-wis.
May nought helpe elles; for wite thou
this:
If thou fle it, it shal flee thee;
Folowe it, and folowen shal it thee."

Whanne I hadde herde all Resoun seyne,
Which hadde spilt hir speche in veyne,
"Dame," seide I, "I dar wel sey,
Of this avaunt me wel I may,
That from youre scole so devyaunt
I am, that never the more avaunt
Right nought am I thurgh youre
doctrine.
I dulle under youre discipline,
I wote no more than wist [I] ever;
To me so contrarie and so fer
Is every thing that ye me lere,
And yit I can it all by *par cuer*,
Myne herte foryetith therof right
nought,
It is so writen in my thought;
And depe greven it is so tendir
That all by herte I can it rendre,
And rede it over comunely;
But to my-silf lewedist am I.
But sith ye love discreven so,
And lak and preise it bothe twoo,
Defyneth it into this letter
That I may thenke on it the better;
For I herde never diffyne it ere,
And wilfully I wolde it lere."

Raisoun. "If love be serched wel and
sought,
It is a sykenesse of the thought,
Annexed and knet bitwixe tweyne
Which male and female with oo cheyne
So frely byndith that they nyll twynne,
Whether so therof they leese or wynne.
The roote springith thurgh hoote
brennyng
Into disordinat desiryng
Forto kissen and enbrace,
And at her lust them to solace;
Of other thyng love recchith nought
But setteth her herte and all her thought,
More for delectacioun
Than ony procreacioun
Of other fruyt by engendrure;
(Which love to god is not plesure),
For of her body fruyt to gete
They yeve no force, they are so sette
Upon delite to pley in-feere.
And somme have also this manere,
To feynen hem for love seke.
Sich love I preise not at a leke,
For paramours they do but feyne,
To love truly they disdeyne;
They falsen ladies traitoursly,
And swerne hem othes utterly,
With many a lesyng and many a fable,
And all they fynden deceyvable;
And whanne they han her lust [y]geten,
The hoote ernes they al foryeten.
Wymmen the harme they bien full sore
But men this thenken evermore;
That lasse harme is, so mote I the,
Deceyve them than deceyved be;
And namely where they ne may
Fynde none other mene wey.
For I wote wel, in sothfastnesse,
What wight doth now his bisynesse
With ony womman forto dele

For ony lust that he may fele,
But if it be for engendrure,
He doth trespasse, I you ensure.
For he shulde setten all his wille
To geten a likly thyng hym tille,
And to sustene, if he myght,
And kepe forth, by kyndes right,
His owne lyknesse and semblable.
For because all is corumpable,
And faile shulde successioun,
Ne were ther generacioun
Oure sectis strene forto save,
Whanne fader or moder arn in grave,
Her children shulde, whanne they ben deede,
Full diligent ben in her steede
To use that werke on such a wise,
That oon may thurgh another rise.
Therfore sette Kynde therynne delite;
For men therynne shulde hem delite,
And of that deede be not erke,
But ofte sithes haunt that werke.
For noon wolde drawe therof a draught,
Ne were delite which hath hym kaught.
Thus hath sotilled Dame Nature;
For noon goth right, I thee ensure,
Ne hath entent hool ne parfit,
For hir desir is for delyte;
The which for tene crece, and eke
The pley of love for-ofte seke,
And thrall hem silf they be so nyce
Unto the prince of every vyce;
For of ech synne it is the rote
Unlefull lust, though it be sote,
And of all yvell the racyne,
As Tulius can determyne
(Which in his tyme was full sage,)
In a boke he made OF AGE,
Where that more he preyseth eelde,
Though he be croked and unweelde,
And more of commendacioun
Than youthe in his discripcioun,
For youthe sette bothe man and wyf
In all perell of soule and lyf,
And perell is, but men have grace,
The perell of yougth[e] forto pace
Withoute ony deth or distresse,
It is so full of wyldenesse.
So ofte it doth shame or damage
To hym, or to his lynage.
It ledith man now up, now doun,
In mochel dissolucioun,
And makith hym love yvell companye,
And lede his lyf disrewlilye,
And halt hym payed with noon estate.
Withynne hym-silf is such debate,
He chaungith purpos and entente
And yalte [him] into somme covente,
To lyven aftir her emprise,
And lesith fredom and fraunchise,
That nature in hym hadde sette.
The which ageyne he may not gette,
If he there make his mansioun,
For to abide professioun.
Though for a tyme his herte absente,
It may not fayle, he shal repente,
And eke abide thilke day
To leve his abite and gone his way;
And lesith his worship and his name,
And dar not come ageyn for shame,
But al his lyf he doth so morne,
By cause he dar not hom retourne.
Fredom of kynde so lost hath he,
That never may recured be,
But that if God hym graunte grace
That he may, er he hennes pace,
Conteyne undir obedience
Thurgh the vertu of pacience.

For youthe sett man in all folye,
In unthrift and [in] ribaudie,
In leccherie and in outrage,
So ofte it chaungith of corage.
Youthe gynneth ofte sich bargeyne
That may not eende withouten peyne.
In gret perell is sett youthede,
Delite so doth his bridil leede.
Delite thus hangith, drede thee nought,
Bothe mannys body and his thought
Oonly thurgh youth, [his] chamberere,
That to done yvell is custommere,
And of nought elles taketh hede
But oonly folkes forto lede
Into disporte and wyldenesse,
So [she] is frowarde from sadnesse.
But Eelde drawith hem therfro,
Who wote it nought, he may wel goo
And moo of hem that now arn olde,
That whilom youthhed hadde in holde,
Which yit remembre of tendir age,
How it hem brought in many a rage,
And many a foly therynne wrought.
But now that Eelde hath hem thourgh sought,
They repente hem of her folye,
That youthe hem putte in jupardye,
In perell, and in myche woo,
And made hem ofte amys to do,
And suen yvell companye,
Riot and avouterie.

But Eelde can ageyn restreyne
From sich folye, and refreyne
And sette men by her ordinaunce
In good reule and in governaunce.
But yvell she spendith hir servise
For no man wole hir love ne preise,
She is hated, this wote I welle,
Hir acqueyntaunce wolde noman fele
Ne han of Elde companye,
Men hate to be of hir alye;
For noman wolde bicomen olde
Ne dye, whanne he is yong and bolde.
And Eelde merveilith right gretlye,
Whanne thei remembre hem inwardly,
Of many a perelous emprise,
Whiche that they wrought in sondry wise
How evere they myght, withoute blam
Escape awey withoute shame.
In youthe withoute damage
Or repreef of her lynage,
Losse of membre, shedyng of blode,
Perell of deth, or losse of good.
Woste thou nought where Youthe abit,
That men so preisen in her witt?
With Delite she halt sojour,
For bothe they dwellen in oo tour.
As longe as Youthe is in sesoun
They dwellen in oon mansioun.
Delite of Youthe wole have servise
To do what so he wole devise;
And Youthe is redy evermore
Forto obey for smerte of sore
Unto Delite, and hym to yive
Hir servise while that she may lyve.
Where Elde abit I wole thee telle
Shortly, and no while dwelle,
For thidir byhoveth thee to goo.
If deth in youthe [hath] thee not sloo,
Of this journey thou maist not faile.
With hir Labour and Travaile
Logged ben, with Sorwe and Woo
That never out of hir court goo.
Peyne and Distresse, Syknesse and Ire
And Malencoly, that angry sire,
Ben of hir paleys senatours;
Gronyng and Grucchyng hir herbejours

YOUTHE AND DELITE

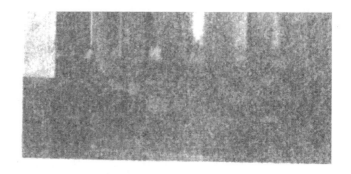

YOUTHE AND DELITE

Or repreef of her lynage,
Losse of membre, shedyng of blode,
Perell of deth, or losse of good.
Woste thou nought where Youthe abit,
That men so preisen in her witt?
With Delite she halt sojour,
For bothe they dwellen in oo tour.
As longe as Youthe is in sesoun
They dwellen in oon mansioun.
Delite of Youthe wole have servise
To do what so he wole devise;
And Youthe is redy evermore
Forto obey for smerte of sore
Unto Delite, and hym to yive
Hir servise while that she may lyve.
Where Elde abit I wole thee telle
Shortly, and no while dwelle,
For thidir byhoveth thee to goo.
If deth in youthe [hath] thee not sloo
Of this journey thou maist not faile.
With hir Labour and Travaile
Logged ben, with Sorwe and Woo
That never out of hir court goo.
Peyne and Distresse, Syknesse and Ire
And Malencoly, that angry sire,
Ben of hir paleys senatours;
Gronyng and Grucchyng hir herbejours

The day and nyght hir to turment,
With cruell deth they hir present;
And tellen hir, erliche and late,
That Deth stont armed at hir gate.
Thanne brynge they to her remembraunce
The foly dedis of hir infaunce,
Whiche causen hir to mourne in woo
That Youthe hath hir bigiled so,
Which sodeynly awey is hasted.
She wepeth the tyme that she hath wasted,
Compleynyng of the preterit
And the present, that not abit,
And of hir olde vanite;
That, but aforn hir she may see
In the future somme socour,
To leggen hir of hir dolour,
To graunte hir tyme of repentaunce,
For her synnes to do penaunce,
And at the laste so hir governe
To wynne the joy that is eterne,
Fro which go bakward Youthe her made
In vanite to droune and wade,—
For present tyme abidith nought,
It is more swift than any thought,
So litel while it doth endure
That ther nys compte ne mesure.
But how that evere the game go
Who list to have joie and mirth also
Of love, be it he or she
High or lowe, who it be,
In fruyt they shulde hem delyte;
Her part they may not elles quyte,
To save hem-silf in honeste.
And yit full many one I se
Of wymmen, sothly forto seyne,
That desire and wolde fayne
The pley of love, they be so wilde,
And not coveite to go with childe.
And if with child they be perchaunce,
They wole it holde a gret myschaunce;
But what-som-ever woo they fele,
They wole not pleyne but concele,
But if it be ony fool or nyce
In whom that Shame hath no justice.
For to delyte echone they drawe,
That haunte this werke bothe high and lawe,
Save sich that arn worth right nought
That for money wole be bought.
Such love I preise in no wise,
Whanne it is goven for coveitise.
I preise no womman though she be wood
That yeveth hir-silf for ony good.
For litel shulde a man telle,
Of hir that wole hir body selle,
Be she mayde, be she wyf,
That quyk wole selle hir, bi hir lif.
How faire chere that evere she make
He is a wrecche, I undirtake,
That loved such one, for swete or soure,
Though she hym calle hir paramoure,
And laugheth on hym, and makith hym feeste;
For certeynly no such beeste
To be loved is not worthy,
Or bere the name of druerie.
Noon shulde hir please, but he were woode,
That wole dispoile hym of his goode.
Yit nevertheles I wole not sey
That she for solace and for pley
Ne may a jewel or other thyng
Take of her loves fre yevyng;
But that she aske it in no wise,
For drede of shame of coveitise.
And she of hirs may hym certeyn
Withoute sclaundre yeven ageyn,
And joyne her hertes to-gidre so

In love, and take and yeve also.
Trowe not that I wolde hem twynne
Whanne in her love ther is no synne;
I wole that they to-gedre go,
And don al that they han ado,
As curteis shulde and debonaire,
And in her love beren hem faire,
Withoute vice, bothe he and she,
So that alwey in honeste
Fro foly love they kepe hem clere,
That brenneth hertis with his fere,
And that her love in ony wise
Be devoide of coveitise.
Good love shulde engendrid be
Of trewe herte, just and secre,
And not of such as sette her thought
To have her lust, and ellis nought.
So are they caught in loves lace,
Truly for bodily solace.
Fleshly delite is so present
With thee, that sette all thyne entent,
Withoute more (what shulde I glose?)
Forto gete and have the Rose,
Which makith [thee] so mate and woode,
That thou desirest noon other goode.
But thou art not an inche the nerre,
But evere abidist in sorwe and werre,
As in thi face it is sene;
It makith thee bothe pale and lene;
Thy myght, thi vertu goth away.
A sory geste, in goode fay,
Thou herberest then in thyne inne,
The God of Love whanne thou let inne.
Wherfore I rede thou shette hym oute,
Or he shall greve thee, oute of doute;
For to thi profit it wole turne,
Iff he nomore with thee sojourne.
In gret myscheef and sorwe sonken
Ben hertis that of love arn dronken,
As thou peraunter knowen shall
Whanne thou hast lost thi tyme all,
And spent thy youth in ydilnesse
In waste and wofull lustynesse
If thow maist lyve the tyme to se
Of love forto delyvered be,
Thy tyme thou shalt biwepe sore,
The whiche never thou maist restore,
For tyme lost, as men may see,
For no thyng may recured be.
And if thou scape yit atte laste
Fro Love that hath thee so faste
Knytt and bounden in his lace,
Certeyn I holde it but a grace.
For many oon, as it is seyne,
Have lost and spent also in veyne
In his servise, withoute socour,
Body and soule, good and tresour,
Witte and strengthe and eke richesse,
Of which they hadde never redresse."

Thus taught and preched hath resoun,
But Love spilte hir sermoun,
That was so ymped in my thought,
That hir doctrine I sette at nought.
And yitt ne seide she never a dele
That I ne undirstode it wele,
Word by word the mater all;
But unto love I was so thrall,
Which callith over-all his pray,
He chasith so my thought al day,
And halt myne herte undir his sele,
As trust and trew as ony stele.
So that no devocioun
Ne hadde I in the sermoun
Of dame Resoun, ne of hir rede.
It toke no sojour in myne hede,
For all yede oute at [that] oon ere,
That in that other she dide lere;

Fully on me she lost hir lore.
Hir speche me greved wondir sore.

Than unto hir for ire I seide,
For anger as I dide abraide:
Dame, and is it youre wille algate
That I not love, but that I hate
Alle men, as ye me teche?
For if I do aftir youre speche,
Sith that ye seyne love is not good,
Thanne must I nedis say with mood,
f I it leve, in hatrede ay
To lyven, and voide love away
From me, [and be] a synfull wrecche,
Hated of all that [love that] tecche;
may not go noon other gate,
For other must I love or hate.
And if I hate men of newe
More than love, it wole me rewe,
As by youre preching semeth me,
For Love no thing ne preisith thee.
Ye yeve good counsel sikirly,
That prechith me al day that I
hulde not loves lore alowe,
He were a foole wolde you not trowe.
n speche also ye han me taught
Another love that knowen is naught,
Which I have herd you not repreve,
To love ech other. By youre leve,
f ye wolde diffyne it me,
wolde gladly here to se,
Atte the leest, if I may lere,
Of sondry loves the manere."
Raisoun. "Certis freend a fool art thou
Whan that thou no thyng wolt allowe,
That I for thi profit say.
Yit wole I sey thee more in fay,
For I am redy at the leste
To accomplisshe thi requeste.
But I not where it wole avayle,
In veyn perauntre I shal travayle.
Love ther is in sondry wise,
As I shal thee heere devise
For somme love leful is and good;
I mene not that which makith thee wood,
And bringith thee in many a fitte
And ravysshith fro thee al thi witte,
It is so merveilouse and queynte;
With such love be no more aqueynte.

Love of freendship also ther is,
Which makith no man done amys,
Of wille knytt bitwixe two,
That wole not breke for wele ne woo;
Which long is likly to contune
Whanne wille and goodis ben in comune;
Grounded by goddis ordinaunce,
Hoole withoute discordaunce;
With hem holdyng comunte
Of all her goode in charite;
That ther be noon excepcioun
Thurgh chaungyng of entencioun;
That ech helpe other at her neede,
And wisely hele bothe word and dede;
Trewe of menyng, devoide of slouthe,
For witt is nought withoute trouthe,
So that the ton dar all his thought,
Seyn to his freend and spare nought
As to hym silf, withoute dredyng
To be discovered by wreying.
For glad is that conjunccioun
Whanne ther is noon susspecioun,
[Ne lak in hem] whom they wolde prove,
That trewe and parfit weren in love.
For no man may be amyable,
But if he be so ferme and stable
That fortune chaunge hym not, ne blynde;

But that his freend all-wey hym fynde,
Bothe pore and riche, in oon estate.
For if his freend, thurgh ony gate,
Wole compleyne of his poverte,
He shulde not bide so long til he
Of his helpyng hym requere;
For goode dede done thurgh praiere
Is sold and bought to deere, I-wys,
To hert that of grete valour is.
For hert fulfilled of gentilnesse
Can yvel demene his distresse,
And man, that worthy is of name,
To asken often hath gret shame.
A good man brenneth in his thought
For shame, whanne he axeth ought.
He hath gret thought, and dredeth ay
For his disese, whanne he shal pray
His freend, lest that he warned be,
Til that he preve his stabilte.
But whanne that he hath founden oon,
That trusty is and trewe as stone,
And [hath] assaied hym at alle,
And founde hym stedefast as a walle
And of his freendship be certeyne,
He shal hym shewe bothe joye and peyne,
And all that [he] dar thynke or sey,
Withoute shame, as he wel may.
For how shulde he a-shamed be
Of sich one as I tolde thee?
For whanne he woot his secre thought,
The thridde shal knowe therof right
nought;
For tweyne of noumbre is bet than thre
In every counsell and secre.
Repreve he dredeth never a deele
Who that bisett his wordis wele.
For every wise man, out of drede,
Can kepe his tunge till he se nede;
And fooles can not holde her tunge—
'A fooles belle is soone runge.'
Yit shal a trewe freend do more,
To helpe his felowe of his sore,
And socoure hym, whanne he hath neede,
In all that he may done in deede;
And gladder [be] that he hym plesith,
Than his felowe, that he esith.
And if he do not his requeste,
He shal as mochel hym moleste
As his felow, for that he
May not fulfille his volunte
Fully, as he hath requered.
If bothe the hertis Love hath fered,
Joy and woo they shull departe
And take evenly ech his parte;
Half his anoy he shal have ay,
And comfort [him] what that he may;
And of his blisse parte shal he,
If love wel departed be.

And whilom of this unyte
Spake Tulius in a ditee,
Man shulde maken his requeste
Unto his freend that is honeste,
And he goodly shulde it fulfille,
But if the more were out of skile;
And other wise not graunte therto,
Except oonly in causes twoo;
If men his freend to deth wolde drive,
Late hym be bisy to save his lyve;
Also if men wolen hym assayle
Of his wurship to make hym faile,
And hyndren hym of his renoun;
Late hym, with full entencioun,
His dever done in eche degre
That his freend ne shamed be,
In this two causes with his myght,
Taking no kepe to skile nor right
As ferre as love may hym excuse;

This ought no man to refuse.
This love, that I have tolde to thee,
Is no thing contrarie to me;
This wole I that thou folowe wele,
And leve the tother everydele;
This love to vertu all entendith,
The tothir fooles blent and shendith.

Another love also there is,
That is contrarie unto this;
Which desire is so constreyned
That [it] is but wille feyned.
Awey fro trouthe it doth so varie,
That to good love it is contrarie,
For it maymeth in many wise
Sike hertis with coveitise.
All in wynnyng and in profit
Sich love settith his delite.
This love so hangeth in balaunce,
That if it lese his hope perchaunce
Of lucre that he is sett upon,
It wole faile and quenche anoon.
For no man may be amerous,
Ne in his lyvyng vertuous,
But he love more in moode
Men for him-silf than for her goode.
For love that profit doth abide
Is fals, and bit not in no tyde
[This] love cometh of Dame Fortune,
That litel while wole contune;
For it shal chaungen wonder soone,
And take Eclips; right as the moone
Whanne he is from us lett
Thurgh erthe, that bitwixe is sett
The sonne and hir, as it may falle,
Be it in partie or in all.
The shadowe maketh her bemys merke,
And hir hornes to shewe derke
That part where she hath lost hir lyght
Of Phebus fully, and the sight;
Til, whanne the shadowe is overpaste,
She is enlumyned ageyn as faste
Thurgh the brightnesse of the sonne bemes,
That yeveth to hir ageyne hir lemes.
That love is right of sich nature,
Now is faire, and now obscure,
Now bright, now clipsi of manere,
And whilom dymme, and whilom clere.
As soone as poverte gynneth take,
With mantel and [with] wedis blake
Hidith of love the light awey,
That into nyght it turneth day;
It may not see richesse shyne,
Till the blake shadowes fyne.
For whanne richesse shyneth bright
Love recovereth ageyn his light,
And whanne it failith, he wole flit;
And as she groweth, so groweth it.
Of this love here what I sey:
The riche men are loved ay,
And namely tho that sparand bene,
That wole not wasshe her hertes clene
Of the filthe, nor of the vice
Of gredy brennyng avarice.
The riche man full fonned is y-wys,
That weneth that he loved is;
If that his herte it undirstode,
It is not he, it is his goode;
He may wel witen in his thought
His good is loved and he right nought.
For if he be a nygard eke,
Men wole not sette by hym a leke,
But haten hym, this is the sothe.
Lo, what profit his catell doth?
Of every man that may hym see,
It geteth hym nought but enmyte.
But he amende hym of that vice,

And knowe hym silf, he is not wys.
Certys he shulde ay freendly be,
To gete hym love also ben free,
Or ellis he is not wise ne sage,
Nomore than is a gote ramage.

That he not loveth his dede proveth,
Whan he his richesse so wel loveth
That he wole hide it ay and spare,
His pore freendis sene forfare
To kepen alway his purpose,
Til for drede his yen close,
And til a wikked deth hym take.
Hym hadde lever a-sondre shake
And late hise lymes a-sondre ryve,
Than leve his richesse in his lyve;
He thenkith parte it with no man.
Certayn no love is in hym than;
How shulde love withynne hym be,
Whanne in his herte is no pite?
That he trespasseth wel I wat,
For ech man knowith his estate.
For wel hym ought to be reproved
That loveth nought, ne is not loved.
But sen we arn to fortune comen,
And hath oure sermoun of hir nomen,
A wondir will y telle thee nowe;
Thou herdist never sich oon I trowe
I note where thou me leven shall,
Though sothfastnesse it be at all.
As it is writen and is soth,
That unto men more profit doth
The froward fortune and contraire,
Than the swote and debonaire;
And if thee thynke it is doutable
It is thurgh argument provable;
For the debonaire and softe
Falsith and bigilith ofte.
For lyche a moder she can cherishe,
And mylken [hem] as doth a norys;
And of hir goode to hem deles,
And yeveth hem parte of her joweles,
With grete richesse and dignite;
And hem she hoteth stabilite
In a state that is not stable,
But chaungynge ay and variable;
And fedith hym with glorie veyne,
In worldly blisse noncerteyne.
Whanne she hem settith on hir whele
Thanne wene they to be right wele,
And in so stable state withall
That never they wene forto falle.
And whanne they sette so highe be,
They wene to have in certeynte
Of hertly freendis so grete noumbre
That nothyng myght her state encombre
They trust hem so on every side,
Wenyng with hem they wolde abide
In every perell and myschaunce,
Withoute chaunge or variaunce
Bothe of catell and of goode.
And also forto spende her bloode,
And all her membris forto spille,
Oonly to fulfille her wille.
They maken it hole in many wise,
And hoten hem her full servise,
How sore that it do hem smerte,
Into her naked sherte.
Herte and all so hole they yive,
For the tyme that they may lyve.
So that with her flaterie,
They maken foolis glorifie
Of her wordis spekyng,
And han ther-of a rejoysyng,
And trowe hem as the Evangile:
And it is all falsheede and gile,
As they shal aftirwarde se
Whanne they arn falle in poverte,

And ben of good and catell bare;
Thanne shulde they sene who freendis ware.
For of an hundred certeynly,
Nor of a thousande full scarsly,
Ne shal they fynde unnethis oon
Whanne poverte is comen upon.
For this Fortune that I of telle
With men whanne hir lust to dwelle,
Makith hem to leese her conisaunce,
And norishith hem in ignoraunce.

But froward Fortune and perverse,
Whanne high estatis she doth reverse,
And maketh hem to tumble doune
Of hir whele, with sodeyn tourne,
And from her richesse doth hem fle,
And plongeth hem in poverte,
As a stepmoder envyous
And leieth a plastre dolorous
Unto her hertis wounded egre,
Which is not tempred with vynegre
But with poverte and indigence—
Forto shewe by experience
That she is Fortune verelye,
In whom no man shulde affye,
Nor in hir yeftis have fiaunce,
She is so full of variaunce.
Thus kan she maken high and lowe,
Whanne they from richesse arn [y-] throwe,
Fully to knowen without were
Freend of affect and freend of chere;
And which in love were trewe and stable,
And whiche also were variable,
After Fortune her goddesse,
In poverte outher in richesse.
For all she yeveth here, out of drede,
Unhappe bereveth it in dede;
For in-fortune late not oon
Of freendis, whanne Fortune is gone—
I mene tho freendis that wole fle
Anoon, as entreth poverte;
And yit they wole not leve hem so,
But in ech place where they go,
They calle hem 'wrecche,' scorne, and blame,
And of her myshappe hem diffame.
And namely siche as in richesse
Pretendid moost of stablenesse,
Whanne that they sawe hym sette on lofte,
And were of hym socoured ofte,
And most yholpe in all her neede;
But now they take no maner heede,
But seyn in voice of flaterie,
That now apperith her folye
Over-all where so they fare,
And synge 'Go fare-wel, feldefare.'
All suche freendis I beshrewe,
For of trewe ther be to fewe.
But sothfast freendis, what so bitide,
In every fortune wolen abide;
Thei han her hertis in suche noblesse
That they nyl love for no richesse,
Nor for that fortune may hem sende
Thei wolen hem socoure and defende,
And chaunge for softe ne for sore;
For who is freend loveth evermore.
Though men drawe swerde his freend to slo,
He may not hewe her love a-two,
But in case that I shall sey;
For pride and ire lese it he may,
And for reprove by nycete,
And discovering of privite;
With tonge woundyng as feloun,
Thurgh venemous detraccioun.
Frende in this case wole gone his way,

For no thyng greve hym more ne may,
And for nought ellis wole he fle,
If that he love in stabilite.
And certeyn he is wel bigone,
Among a thousand that fyndith oon;
For ther may be no richesse
Ageyns frendshipp of worthynesse;
For it ne may so high atteigne
As may the valoure, soth to seyne,
Of hym that loveth trew and well.
Frendshipp is more than is catell,
For freend in court ay better is,
Than peny in purs certis
And Fortune myshappyng,
Whanne upon men she is fallyng
Thurgh mysturnyng of hir chaunce,
And casteth hem oute of balaunce,
She makith thurgh hir adversite
Men full clerly forto se
Hym that is freend in existence,
From hym that is by apparence.
For yn-fortune makith anoon,
To knowe thy freendis fro thy foon,
By experience right as it is.
The which is more to preise y-wis,
Than is myche richesse and tresour.
For more dothe profit and valour
Poverte and such adversite
Bi fer than doth prosperite;
For the toon yeveth conysaunce,
And the tother ignoraunce.

And thus in poverte is in dede
Trouthe declared fro falsheed,
For feynte frendis it wole declare,
And trewe also what wey they fare.
For whanne he was in his richesse,
These freendis ful of doublenesse
Offrid hym in many wise
Hert, and body, and servise;
What wolde he thanne ha yove to ha
bought
To knowen openly her thought,
That he now hath so clerly seen?
The lasse bigiled he shulde have bene,
And he hadde thanne perceyved it;
But richesse nold not late hym witte.
Wel more avauntage doth hym thanne,
Sith that it makith hym a wise man,
The gret myscheef that he receyveth,
Than doth richesse that hym deceyveth.
Richesse riche ne makith nought
Hym that on tresour sette his thought;
For richesse stonte in suffisaunce
And no-thyng in habundaunce;
For suffisaunce all oonly
Makith men to lyve richely.
For he that at mycches tweyne,
Ne valued [is] in his demeine,
Lyveth more at ese, and more is riche,
Than doth he that is chiche,
And in his berne hath, soth to seyn,
An hundred mowis of whete greyne,
Though he be chapman or marchaunte,
And have of golde many [a] besaunte.
For in the getyng he hath such woo,
And in the kepyng drede also,
And sette evermore his bisynesse
Forto encrese, and not to lesse,
Forto aument and multiplie.
And though on hepis that lye hym bye,
Yit never shal make his richesse
Asseth unto his gredynesse.
But the povere that recchith nought,
Save of his lyflode, in his thought,
Which that he getith with his travaile,
He dredith nought that it shall faile,
Though he have lytel worldis goode,

Mete, and drynke, and esy foode,
Upon his travel and lyvyng,
And also suffisaunt clothyng.
Or if in syknesse that he fall,
And lothe mete and drynke withall,
Though he have not his mete to bye
He shal bithynke hym hastily
To putte hym oute of all daunger,
That he of mete hath no myster;
Or that he may with lytel eke
Be founden, while that he is seke;
Or that men shull hym berne in haste,
To lyve til his syknesse be paste,
To somme maysondewe biside;
Or he caste nought what shal hym
bitide—
He thenkith nought that evere he shall
Into ony sykenesse fall.
And though it falle, as it may be,
That all be-tyme spare shall he
As mochel, as shal to hym suffice
While he is sike in ony wise,
He doth [that] for that he wole be
Contente with his poverte,
Withoute nede of ony man.
So myche in litel have he can,
He is apaied with his fortune;
And for he nyl be importune
Unto no wight, ne honerous,
Nor of her goodes coveitous,
Therfore he spareth, it may wel bene,
His pore estate forto sustene.
Or if hym lust not forto spare,
But suffrith forth as not ne ware,
Atte last it hapneth as it may
Right unto his laste day,
And taketh the world as it wolde be;
For evere in herte thenkith he,
The sonner that [the] deth hym slo,
To paradys the sonner go
He shal, there forto lyve in blisse,
Where that he shal noo good misse;
Thider he hopith God shal hym sende,
Aftir his wrecchid lyves ende.
Pictagoras hym silf reherses
In a book, that the Golden Verses
Is clepid for the nobilite
Of the honourable ditee,
That whanne thou goste thy body fro,
Fre in the eir thou shalt up go,
And leven al humanite,
And purely lyve in deite.
He is a foole withouten were
That trowith have his Countre heere;
In erthe is not oure Countre—
That may these clerkis seyn, and see
In Boice of Consolacioun,
Where it is maked mencioun
Of oure countre pleyn at the ye
By teching of Philosophie;
Where lewid men myght lere witte,
Who so that wolde translaten it.
If he be sich that can wel lyve
Aftir his rente may hym yive,
And not desireth more to have,
Than may fro poverte hym save.
A wise man seide, as we may seen,
Is no man wrecche but he it wene,
Be he kyng, knyght, or ribaude;
And many a ribaude is mery and baude
That swynkith and berith bothe day
and nyght
Many a burthen of gret myght,
The whiche doth hym lasse offense
For he suffrith in pacience.
They laugh and daunce, trippe and synge,
And ley not up for her lyvyng,
But in the taverne all dispendith

The wynnyng that God hem sendith.
Thanne goth he fardeles forto bere,
With as good chere as he dide ere;
To swynke and traveile he not feynith,
For for to robben he disdeynith;
But right anoon aftir his swynke
He goth to taverne forto drynke.
All these ar riche in abundaunce,
That can thus have suffisaunce
Wel more than can an usurere,
As God wel knowith, withoute were.
For an usurer, so God me se,
Shal nevere for richesse riche be,
But evermore pore and indigent,
Scarce and gredy in his entent.

For soth it is, whom it displese,
Ther may no marchaunt lyve at ese.
His herte in sich a werre is sett,
That it quyk brenneth more to gete,
Ne never shal enough have geten,
Though he have gold in gerners yeten.
Forto be nedy he dredith sore,
Wherfore to geten more and more
He sette his herte and his desire.
So hote he brennyth in the fire,
Of coveitise, that makith hym woode
To purchace other mennes goode.
He undirfongith a gret peyne
That undirtakith to drynke up Seyne;
For the more he drynkith ay
The more he leveth, the soth to say.
Thus is thurst of fals getyng,
That laste ever in coveityng,
And the angwisshe and distresse,
With the fire of gredynesse.
She fightith with hym ay and stryveth,
That his herte a-sondre ryveth;
Such gredynesse hym assaylith,
That whanne he most hath, most he failith
Phisiciens and advocates
Gone right by the same yates;
They selle her science for wynnyng,
And haunte her crafte for gret getyng.
Her wynnyng is of such swetnesse,
That if a man falle in sikenesse,
They are full glad for ther encrese;
For by her wille, withoute lees,
Everiche man shulde be seke,
And though they die, they sette not a lek
After, whanne they the gold have take,
Full litel care for hem they make;
They wolde that fourty were seke atonys—
Ye ii hundred in flesh and bonys,
And yit ii thousand, as I gesse,
Forto encrecen her richesse.
They wole not worchen in no wise,
But for lucre and coveitise.
For Fysic gynneth first by 'Fy'
(The Phisicien also sothely);
And sithen it goth fro 'Fy' to 'Sy,'
To truste on hem [it] is foly,
For they nyl, in no maner gre,
Do right nought for charite.

Eke in the same secte ar sette
All tho that prechen forto gete
Worshipes, honour, and richesse.
Her hertis arn in grete distresse,
That folk [ne] lyve not holily.
But aboven all specialy
Sich as prechen [in] veynglorie,
And toward god have no memorie,
But forth as ypocrites trace,
And to her soules deth purchace
An outward shewing holynesse,
Though they be full of cursidnesse,

Not liche to the apostles twelve.
They deceyve other and hem selve;
Bigiled is the giler thanne,
For prechyng of a cursed man
Though [it] to other may profite,
Hymsilf it vaileth not a myte.
For ofte goode predicacioun
Cometh of evel entencioun.
To hym not vailith his preching,
All helpe he other with his teching.
For where they good ensaumple take,
There is he with veynglorie shake.
But late us leven these prechoures,
And speke of hem that in her toures
Hepe up her gold, and faste shette,
And sore theron her herte sette.
They neither love God ne drede,
They kepe more than it is nede,
And in her bagges sore it bynde;
Out of the sonne, and of the wynde,
They putte up more than nede ware.
Whanne they seen pore folk forfare,
For hunger die, and for cold quake,
God can wel vengeaunce therof take.
Thre gret myscheves hem assailith,
And thus in gadring ay travaylith:
With mychel peyne they wynne richesse,
And drede hem holdith in distresse
To kepe that they gadre faste,
With sorwe they leve it at the laste;
With sorwe they bothe dye and lyve
That unto richesse her hertis yive.
And in defaute of love it is,
As it shewith ful wel I-wys;
For if this gredy, the sothe to seyn,
Loveden and were loved ageyn,
And goode Love regned over-all,
Such wikkidnesse ne shulde fall.
But he shulde yeve, that most good hadde,
To hem that weren in nede bistadde;
And lyve withoute false usure,
For charite, full clene and pure.
If they hem yeve to goodnesse,
Defendyng hem from ydelnesse,
In all this world thanne pover noon
We shulde fynde, I trowe not oon.
But chaunged is this world unstable,
For love is over-all vendable;
We se that no man loveth nowe,
But for wynnyng and for prowe.
And love is thralled in servage,
Whanne it is sold for avauntage;
Yit wommen wole her bodyes selle—
Suche soules goth to the devel of helle.

. . . .

Whanne Love hadde told hem his entent,
The baronage to councel went;
In many sentences they fille,
And dyversly they seide hir wille.
But aftir discorde they accorded,
And her accord to Love recorded:
"Sir," seiden they, "we ben atone
Bi evene accorde of everichone,
Outake Richesse al oonly,
That sworne hath ful hauteynly,
That she the castell nyl not assaile,
Ne smyte a stroke in this bataile
With darte ne mace, spere ne knyf,
For man that spekith or berith the lyf,
And blameth youre emprise, I-wys,
And from oure hoost departed is,
Atte lest wey as in this plyte,
So hath she this man in dispite.
For, she seith, he ne loved hir never,
And therfore she wole hate hym evere.
For he wole gadre no tresoure,
He hath hir wrath for evermore;
He agylte hir never in other caas,

Lo, heere all hoolly his trespas.
She seith wel that this other day
He axide hir leve to gone the way
That is clepid 'To-moche-yevyng,'
And spak full faire in his praiyng.
But whanne he praide hir, pore was he,
Therfore she warned hym the entre;
Ne yit is he not thryven so
That he hath geten a peny or two,
That quytly is his owne, in holde.
Thus hath Richesse us all[e] tolde;
And whanne Richesse us this recorded,
Withouten hir we ben accorded.
And we fynde in oure accordaunce
That False-Semblant and Abstinaunce,
With all the folk of her bataille,
Shull at the hyndre gate assayle,
That Wikkid-Tunge hath in kepyng
With his Normans full of janglyng;
And with hem Curtesie and Largesse,
That shull shewe her hardynesse
To the olde wyf, that kepte so harde
Fair-Welcomyng withynne her warde;
Thanne shal Delite and Wel-Heelynge
Fonde Shame adowne to brynge,
With all her oost early and late
They shull assailen that ilke gate;
Agaynes Drede shall Hardynesse
Assayle, and also Sikernesse
With all the folk of her ledyng,
That never wist what was fleyng;
Fraunchise shall fight and eke Pite
With Daunger, full of Cruelte;
Thus is youre hoost ordeyned wele.
Doune shall the castell every-dele,
If everiche do his entent,
So that Venus be present,
Youre modir full of vesselage
That can ynough of such usage.
Withouten hir may no wight spede
This werk, neithir for word ne deede;
Therfore is good ye for hir sende,
For thurgh hir may this werk amende."

"Lordynges, my modir, the goddesse,
That is my lady and my maistresse,
Nis not [at] all at my willyng,
Ne doth not all my desiryng;
Yit can she some tyme done labour,
Whanne that hir lust, in my socour,
As my nede is forto a-cheve.
But now I thenke hir not to geve;
My modir is she, and of childehede,
I bothe worshipe hir and drede
For who that dredith sire ne dame,
Shal it abye in body or name.
And netheles yit kunne we
Sende aftir hir if nede be;
And were she nygh she comen wolde,
I trowe that no thyng myght hir holde.
Mi modir is of gret prowesse,
She hath tan many a forteresse,
That cost hath many a pounde, er this,
There I nas not present y-wis;
And yit men seide it was my dede.
But I come never in that stede,
Ne me ne likith, so mote I the,
That suche toures ben take withoute me,
For why me thenkith that in no wise
It may bene clepid but marchandise.
Go bye a courser, blak or white,
And pay therfore, than art thou quyte;
The marchaunt owith thee right nought,
Ne thou hym, whanne thou it bought,
I wole not sellyng clepe 'yevyng,'
For sellyng axeth no guerdonyng,
Here lith no thank ne no merite;
That oon goth from that other al quyte.

"MI MODIR IS OF GRET PROWESSE"

ne, in holde.
s all[e] tolde;
us this recorded,
accorded.
accordaunce
nd Abstinaunce,
er bataille,
te assayle,
hath in kepyng
l of janglyng;
ie and Largesse,
hardynesse
kepte so harde
ynne her warde;
Wel-Heelynge
to brynge,
and late
at ilke gate;
Hardynesse
nesse
r ledyng,
was fleyng;
and eke Pite
Cruelte;
deyned wele.
every-dele,
nt,
nt,
sselage
[illegible]

Yit can she some tyme done labour,
Whanne that hir lust, in my socour,
As my nede is forto a-cheve.
But now I thenke hir not to geve;
My modir is she, and of childehede,
I bothe worshipe hir and drede.
For who that dredith sire ne dame,
Shal it abye in body or name.
And netheles yit kunne we
Sende aftir hir if nede be;
And were she nygh she comen wolde,
I trowe that no thyng myght hir holde.
Mi modir is of gret prowesse,
She hath tan many a forteresse,
That cost hath many a pounde, er this,
There I nas not present y-wis;
And yit men seide it was my dede.
But I come never in that stede,
Ne me ne likith, so mote I the,
That suche toures ben take withoute me.
For why me thenkith that in no wise
It may bene clepid but marchandise.
Go bye a courser, blak or white,
And pay therfore, than art thou quyte;
The marchaunt owith thee right nought,
Ne thou hym, whanne thou it bought.
I wole not sellyng clepe 'yevyng,'
For sellyng axeth no guerdonyng,
Here lith no thank ne no merite;
That [illegible] that other al quyte

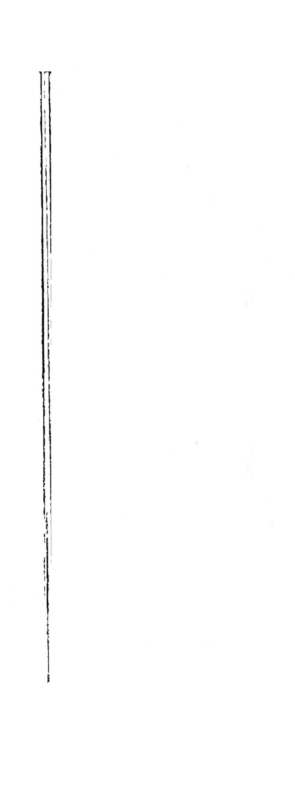

But this sellyng is not semblable;
For whanne his hors is in the stable,
He may it selle ageyn, parde,
And wynnen on it, such happe may be;
All may the man not leese I-wys,
For at the leest the skynne is his.
Or ellis if it so bitide
That he wole kepe his hors to ride,
Yit is he lord ay of his hors.
But thilke chaffare is wel wors,
There Venus entremetith ought.
For who-so such chaffare hath bought,
He shal not worchen so wisely,
That he ne shal leese al outerly
Bothe his money and his chaffare.
But the seller of the ware
The prys and profit have shall,
Certeyn the bier shal leese all.
For he ne can so dere it bye
To have lordship and full maistrie,
Ne have power to make lettyng
Neithir for yift ne for prechyng,
That of his chaffare, maugre his,
Another shal have asmoche, I-wis,
If he wole yeve as myche as he,
Of what contrey so that he be;
Or for right nought, so happe may,
If he can flater hir to hir pay.
Ben thanne siche marchauntz wise?
No but fooles in every wise,
Whanne they bye sich thyng wilfully
There as they leese her good fully.
But natheles this dar I say,
My modir is not wont to pay,
For she is neither so fool ne nyce
To entremete hir of sich vyce.
But trusteth wel he shal pay all,
That repent of his bargeyn shall,
Whanne poverte putte hym in distresse,
All were he scoler to Richesse,
That is for me in gret yernyng
Whanne she assentith to my willyng.
But [by] my modir seint Venus,
And by hir fader Saturnus,
That hir engendride by his lyf
(But not upon his weddid wyf)—
Yit wole I more unto you swere
To make this thyng the sikerere:—
Now by that feith and that leaute
That I owe to all my britheren fre,
Of which ther nys wight undir heven
That kan her fadris names neven,
So dyverse and so many ther be,
That with my modir have be prive;
Yit wolde I swere for sikirnesse,
The pole of helle to my witnesse,
Now drynke I not this yeere clarre,
If that I lye or forsworne be!
(For of the goddes the usage is,
That who so hym forswereth amys
Shal that yeer drynke no clarre.)
Now have I sworne ynough pardee,
If I forswere me, thanne am I lorne—
But I wole never be forsworne.
Syth Richesse hath me failed heere,
She shal abye that trespas dere,
Atte leest wey but hir arme
With swerd, or sparth or [with] gysarme.
For certis sith she loveth not me
Fro thilke tyme that she may se
The castell and the tour to-shake,
In sory tyme she shal awake.
If I may grype a riche man,
I shal so pulle hym, if I can,
That he shal in a fewe stoundes
Lese all his markis and his poundis;
I shal hym make his pens outslynge,
But they in his gerner sprynge.

Oure maydens shal eke pluk hym so,
That hym shal neden fetheres mo,
And make hym selle his londe to spende,
But he the bet kunne hym defende.
Pore men han maad her lord of me;
Al though they not so myghty be
That they may fede me in delite,
I wole not have hem in despite;
No good man hateth hem as I gesse.
For chynche and feloun is richesse;
That so can chase hym and dispise,
And hem defoule in sondry wise.
They loven full bet, so God me spede,
Than doth the riche chynchy gnede;
And ben in goode feith more stable,
And trewer and more serviable.
And therfore it suffisith me
Her goode herte and her leaute.
They han on me sette all her thought,
And therfore I forgete hem nought;
I wolde hem bringe in grete noblesse,
If that I were god of richesse,
As I am god of love sothely,
Sich routhe upon her pleynt have I.
Therfore I must his socour be
That peyneth hym to serven me,
For if he deide for love of this,
Thanne semeth in me no love ther is."

"Sir," seide they, "soth is every deel
That ye reherce, and we wote wel
Thilke oth to holde is resonable.
For it is good and covenable
That ye on riche men han sworne;
For, Sir, this wote we wel biforne:
If Riche men done you homage,
That is, as fooles done, outrage.
But ye shull not forsworen be,
Ne lette, therfore, to drynke clarre
Or pyment makid fresh and newe.
Ladies shull hem such pepir brewe,
If that they fall into her laas,
That they for woo mowe seyn, 'Allas!'
Ladyes shullen evere so curteis be,
That they shal quyte youre oth all free.
Ne sekith never othir vicaire,
For they shal speke with hem so faire,
That ye shal holde you paied full wele,
Though ye you medle never a dele.
Late ladies worche with her thyngis
They shal hem telle so fele tidynges,
And moeve hem eke so many requestis,
Bi flateri, that not honest is;
And therto yeve hym such thankynges,
What with kissyng, and with talkynges,
That certis, if they trowed be,
Shal never leve hem londe ne fee,
That it nyl as the moeble fare
Of which they first delyverid are.
Now may ye telle us all youre wille,
And we youre heestes shal fulfille.

But Fals-Semblaunt dar not for drede
Of you, Sir, medle hym of this dede;
For he seith that ye ben his foo,
He note if ye wole worche hym woo.
Wherfore we pray you alle, Beausire,
That ye forgyve hym now your Ire,
And that he may dwelle as your man
With Abstinence, his dere lemman.
This oure accord and oure wille nowe."
"Parfay," seide Love, "I graunte it yowe;
I wole wel holde hym for my man,
Now late hym come." And he forth ran.
"Fals-Semblant," quod Love, "in this wise
I take thee heere to my servise,

"IF THAT I WERE GOD OF RICHESSE"

ym and dispise,
sondry wise.
, so God me spede,
e chynchy gnede;
eith more stable,
re serviable.
isith me
d her leaute.
te all her thought,
ete hem nought;
in grete noblesse,
f richesse,
sothely,
er pleynt have I.
socour be
to serven me,
ove of this,
ne no love ther is."

oth is every deel
we wote wel
is resonable.
ovenable
en han sworne;
ve wel biforne:
homage,
age.
me,

Late ladies worche with her thyngis
They shal hem telle so fele tidynges,
And moeve hem eke so many requesti
Bi flateri, that not honest is;
And therto yeve hym such thankynge
What with kissyng, and with talkynge
That certis, if they trowed be,
Shal never leve hem londe ne fee,
That it nyl as the moeble fare,
Of which they first delyverid are.
Now may ye telle us all youre wille,
And we youre heestes shal fulfille.

But Fals-Semblaunt dar not for drede
Of you, Sir, medle hym of this dede;
For he seith that ye ben his foo,
He note if ye wole worche hym woo,
Wherfore we pray you alle, Beausire,
That ye forgyve hym now your Ire,
And that he may dwelle as your man
With Abstinence, his dere lemman
This oure accord and oure wille nowe.
"Parfay," seide Love, "I graunte it
yowe;
I wole wel holde hym for my man,
Now late hym come." And he forth r
"Fals-Semblant," quod Love, "in th
wise
I take thee heere to my servise,

That thou oure freendis helpe away,
And hyndreth hem neithir nyght ne day,
But do thy myght hem to releve;
And eke oure enemyes that thou greve;
Thyne be this myght, I graunte it thee,
My Kyng of Harlotes shalt thou be,
We wole that thou have such honour.
Certeyne thou art a fals traitour,
And eke a theef; sith thou were borne,
A thousand tyme thou art forsworne;
But netheles in oure heryng,
To putte oure folk out of doutyng
I bidde thee teche hem, wostowe howe,
Bi somme general signe nowe,
In what place thou shalt founden be,
If that men had myster of thee,
And how men shal thee best espye;
For thee to knowe is gret maistrie.
Telle in what place is thyn hauntyng."
"Sir, I have fele dyverse wonyng,
That I kepe not rehersed be;
So that ye wolde respiten me.
For if that I telle you the sothe,
I may have harme and shame bothe;
If that my felowes wisten it,
My talis shulden me be quytt,
For certeyne they wolde hate me
If ever I knewe her cruelte.
For they wolde overall holde hem stille
Of trouthe that is ageyne her wille;
Suche tales kepen they not here.
I myght eftsoone bye it full deere,
If I seide of hem ony thing
That ought displesith to her heryng.
For what word that hem prikketh or
  biteth,
In that word noon of hem deliteth,
Al were it gospel the Evangile,
That wolde reprove hem of her gile.
For they are cruel and hauteyne,
And this thyng wote I well certeyne;
If I speke ought to peire her loos,
Your court shal not so well be cloos
That they ne shall wite it atte last.
Of good men am I nought agast,
For they wole taken on hem no thyng,
Whanne that they knowe al my menyng.
But he that wole it on hym take,
He wole hym-silf suspecious make
That he his lyf let covertly,
In gile and in Ipocrisie
That me engendred and yaf fostryng."
"They made a full good engendryng,"
Quod Love, "for who so sothly telle,
They engendred the Devel of Helle.
But nedely, how so evere it be,"
Quod Love, "I wole and charge thee
To telle anoon thy wonyng places,
Heryng ech wight that in this place is,
And what lyf that thou lyvest also;
Hide it no lenger now—Wherto?
Thou most discovere all thi wurchyng,
How thou servest, and of what thyng,
Though that thou shuldist for thi
  sothe-sawe
Ben alto beten and to-drawe.
And yit art thou not wont pardee.
But natheles though thou beten be,
Thou shalt not be the first that so
Hath for sothsawe suffred woo."

"Sir, sith that it may liken you,
Though that I shulde be slayne right now,
I shal done youre comaundement,
For therto have I gret talent."
Withouten wordis mo right thanne
Fals-Semblant his sermon biganne,
And seide hem thus in audience:

"Barouns, take heede of my sentence:
That wight that list to have knowing
Of Fals-Semblant, full of flatering,
He must in worldly folk hym seke,
And certes in the cloistres eke,
I wone no where but in hem twey;
But not lyk even, soth to sey.
Shortly, I wole herberwe me
There I hope best to holstred be;
And certeynly sikerest hidyng,
Is undirnethe humblest clothing.
Religiouse folk ben full covert,
Seculer folk ben more appert.
But natheles I wole not blame
Religious folk, ne hem diffame;
In what habit that ever they go,
Religioun umble and trewe also,
Wole I not blame, ne dispise,
But I nyl love it in no wise—
I mene of false religious,
That stoute ben and malicious,
That wolen in an abit goo,
And setten not her herte therto.
Religious folk ben al pitous,
Thou shalt not seen oon dispitous;
They loven no pride, ne no strif,
But humbely they wole lede her lyf.
With which folk wole I never be,
And if I dwelle, I feyne me.
I may wel in her abit go,
But me were lever my nekke a-two
Than lete a purpose that I take,
What covenaunt that ever I make.
I dwelle with hem that proude be,
And full of wiles and subtilte,
That worship of this world coveiten,
And grete nedes kunnen espleiten,
And gone and gadren gret pitaunces,
And purchace hem the acqueyntaunces
Of men that myghty lyf may leden,
And feyne hem pore, and hem silf feden
With gode morcels delicious,
And drinken good wyne precious,
And preche us povert and distresse,
And fisshen hem silf gret richesse
With wily nettis that they cast;
It wole come foule out at the last.
They ben fro clene religioun went,
They make the world an argument,
That [hath] a foule conclusioun:
'I have a robe of religioun,
Thanne am I all religious.'
This argument is all roignous,
It is not worth a croked brere;
Abit ne makith neithir monk ne frere,
But clene lyf and devocioun
Makith gode men of religioun.
Netheles ther kan noon answere,
How high that evere his heed he shere
With rasour whetted never so kene,
That Gile in braunches kut thrittene;
Ther can no wight distincte it so,
That he dare sey a word therto.

But what herberwe that ever I take
Or what Semblant that evere I make,
I mene but gile, and folowe that.
For right no mo than Gibbe oure cat,
That awaiteth myce and rattes to kyllen,
Ne entende I but to bigilen.
Ne no wight may by my clothing
Wite with what folk is my dwellyng,
Ne by my wordis yit, parde,
So softe and so plesaunt they be.
Biholde the dedis that I do,
But thou be blynde thou oughtest so.
For varie her wordis fro her deede,
They thenke on gile withoute dreede,

What maner clothing that they were
Or what estate that evere they bere
Lered or lewde, lord or lady,
Knyght, squyer, burgeis, or bayly."

Right thus while Fals-Semblant sermoneth
Eftsones Love hym aresoneth,
And brake his tale in his spekyng,
As though he had hym tolde lesyng,
And seide, "What Devel is that I here?
What folk hast thou us nempned heere?
May men fynde religioun
In worldly habitacioun?"
"Ye, Sir, it folowith not that they
Shulde lede a wikked lyf, parfey,
Ne not therfore her soules leese,
That hem to worldly clothes chese;
For certis it were gret pitee.
Men may in seculer clothes see
Florishen hooly religioun.
Full many a seynt in feeld and toune,
With many a virgine glorious,
Devoute and full religious
Han deied, that comyn cloth ay beeren,
Yit seyntes nevere the lesse they weren.
I cowde reken you many a ten,
Ye wel nygh [al] these hooly wymmen,
That men in chirchis herie and seke,
Bothe maydens and these wyves eke,
That baren full many a faire child heere,
Wered alwey clothis seculere,
And in the same dieden they,
That seyntes weren, and ben alwey.
The xi. thousand maydens deere,
That beren in heven her ciergis clere,
Of whiche men rede in chirche and synge,
Were take in seculer clothing,
Whanne they resseyved martirdome,
And wonnen hevene unto her home.
Good herte makith the goode thought,
The clothing yeveth ne reveth nought;
The goode thought and the worching
That makith the religioun flowryng—
Ther lyth the goode religioun,
Aftir the right entencioun.

Whoso took a wether's skynne,
And wrapped a gredy wolf therynne
For he shulde go with lambis whyte,
Wenest thou not he wolde hem bite?
Yis, neverthelasse, as he were woode,
He wolde hem wery and drinke ther bloode,
And wel the rather hem disceyve;
For sith they cowde not perceyve
His treget and his cruelte,
They wolde hym folowe al wolde he fle.
If ther be wolves of sich hewe
Amonges these apostlis newe,
Thou, Hooly Chirche, thou maist be wailed,
Sith that thy Citee is assayled
Thourgh knyghtis of thyn owne table.
God wote thi lordship is doutable,
If thei enforce [hem] it to wynne,
That shulde defende it fro withynne.
Who myght defense ayens hem make?
Withoute stroke it mote be take
Of trepeget, or mangonel,
Without displaiyng of pensel.
And if God nyl done it socour,
But lat [it] renne in this colour,
Thou most thyn heestis laten be;
Thanne is ther nought but yelde thee,
Or yeve hem tribute doutelees,
And holde it of hem to have pees.
But gretter harme bitideth thee

That they al maister of it be.
Wel konne they scorne thee withal;
By daye stuffen they the wall,
And al the nyght they mynen there.
Nay, thou planten most elles where
Thyn ympes, if thou wolt fruyt have;
Abide not there thi-silf to save.

But now pees! Heere I turne ageyne,
I wole nomore of this thing seyne,
If I may passen me herby.
I myghte maken you wery;
But I wole heten you al-way
To helpe youre freendis, what I may,
So they wollen my company;
For they be shent al outerly,
But if so falle that I be
Ofte with hem and they with me.
And eke my lemman mote they serve,
Or they shull not my love deserve.
Forsothe I am a fals traitour,
God jugged me for a theef trichour;
Forsworne I am, but wel nygh none
Wote of my gile til it be done.
Thurgh me hath many oon deth resseyved,
That my treget nevere aperceyved;
And yit resseyveth, and shal resseyve,
That my falsnesse shal nevere aperceyve.
But who so doth, if he wise be,
Hym is right good be war of me.
But so sligh is the deceyvyng
That to hard is the aperceyvyng.
For Protheus, that cowde hym chaunge,
In every shap homely and straunge,
Cowde nevere sich gile ne tresoune
As I. For I come never in toune,
There as I myght knowen be;
Though men me bothe myght here and see,
Full wel I can my clothis chaunge,
Take oon and make another straunge.
Now am I knyght, now chasteleyne,
Now prelat, and now chapeleyne,
Now prest, now clerk, and now forstere;
Now am I maister, now scolere,
Now monke, now chanoun, now baily;
What ever myster man am I,
Now am I prince, now am I page,
And kan by herte every langage;
Somme tyme am I hore and olde,
Now am I yonge, [and] stoute, and bolde;
Now am I Robert, now Robyn,
Now Frere Menour, now Iacobyn.
And with me folwith my loteby,
To done me solas and company,
That hight Dame Abstinence-Streyned,
In many a queynte array feyned,
Ryght as it cometh to hir lykyng,
I fulfille al hir desiryng;
Somtyme a wommans cloth take I,
Now am I mayde, now lady;
Somtyme I am religious,
Now lyk an anker in an hous;
Somtyme am I Prioresse,
And now a nonne, and now Abbesse;
And go thurgh alle regiouns,
Sekyng all religiouns.
But to what ordre that I am sworne,
I take the strawe, and lete the corne
To joly folk I enhabite;
I axe nomore but her abite.
What wole ye more? In every wise,
Right as me lyst, I me disgise;
Wel can I wre me undir wede,
Unlyk is my word to my dede.
[I] make into my trappis falle,
Thurgh my pryveleges, alle
That ben in Cristendome alyve,
I may assoile and I may shryve

DAME ABSTINENCE-STREYNED

by.
-ery;
l-way
s, what I may,
npany;
terly,

y with me.
note they serve,
ove deserve.
itour,
eef trichour;
el nygh none
e done.
ondeth resseyved,
aperceyved;
l shal resseyve,
evere aperceyve.
wise be,
war of me.
yvyng
rceyvyng.
le hym chaunge,
nd straunge,
ne tresoune
er in toune.
ven boy
nyght here and see,
his chaunge,

Now am I yonge, [and] stoute, and bolde;
Now am I Robert, now Robyn,
Now Frere Menour, now Iacobyn.
And with me folwith my loteby,
To done me solas and company,
That hight Dame Abstinence-Streyned,
In many a queynte array feyned,
Ryght as it cometh to hir lykyng,
I fulfille al hir desiryng;
Somtyme a wommans cloth take I,
Now am I mayde, now lady;
Somtyme I am religious,
Now lyk an anker in an hous;
Somtyme am I Prioresse,
And now a nonne, and now Abbesse;
And go thurgh alle regiouns,
Sekyng all religiouns.
But to what ordre that I am sworne,
I take the strawe, and lete the corne
To joly folk I enhabite;
I axe nomore but her abite.
What wole ye more? In every wise
Right as me lyst, I me disgise;
Wel can I wre me undir wede,
Unlyk is my word to my dede.
[I] make into my trappis falle,
Thurgh my pryveleges, alle
That ben in Cristendome alyve,
I may assoile and I may shryve

(That no prelat may lette me)
All folk where evere thei founde be;
I note no prelate may done so,
But it the pope be, and no mo,
That made thilk establisshing.
Now is not this a propre thing?
But where my sleight is aperceyved,
Of hem I am nomore resceyved,
As I was wont; and wostow why?
For I dide hem a tregetrie.
But therof yeve I lytel tale;
I have the silver and the male.
So have I prechid, and eke shriven,
So have I take, so have me yiven
Thurgh her foly husbonde and wyf,
That I lede right a joly lyf,
Thurgh symplesse of the prelacye;
They knowe not al my tregettrie.
But for asmoche as man and wyf
Shulde shewe her paroch-prest her lyf
Onys a yeer, as seith the book,
Er ony wight his housel took,
Thanne have I pryvylegis large
That may of myche thing discharge.
For he may seie right thus, parde:—
'Sir Preest, in shrift I telle it thee,
That he to whom that I am shryven
Hath me assoiled, and me yiven
For penaunce sothly for my synne
Which that I fonde me gilty ynne;
Ne I ne have nevere entencioun,
To make double confessioun,
Ne reherce efte my shrift to thee;
O shrift is right ynough to me.
This oughte thee suffice wele,
Ne be not rebel never a dele,
For certis, though thou haddist it sworn,
I wote no prest ne prelat borne
That may to shrift efte me constreyne.
And if they done, I wole me pleyne,
For I wote where to pleyne wele.
Thou shalt not streyne me a dele
Ne enforce me, ne not me trouble
To make my confessioun double.
Ne I have none affeccioun,
To have double absolucioun.
The firste is right ynough to me,
This latter assoilyng quyte I thee.
I am unbounde—What! Maist thou fynde
More of my synnes me to unbynde!
For he that myght hath in his honde
Of all my synnes me unbonde,
And if thou wolt me thus constreyne
That me mote nedis on thee pleyne,
There shall no jugge imperial
Ne bisshop, ne official,
Done jugement on me; for I
Shal gone and pleyne me openly
Unto my shriftefadir newe,
That highte not Frere Wolf untrewe!
And he shal chevys hym for me,
For I trowe he can hampre thee.
But lord! he wolde be wrooth withall,
If men hym wolde Frere Wolf call;
For he wolde have no pacience,
But done al cruel vengeaunce;
He wolde his myght done at the leest
No thing spare, for goddis heest.
And god so wys be my socour,
But thou yeve me my Savyour
At Ester, whanne it likith me,
Withoute presyng more on thee,
I wole forth and to hym gone,
And he shal housel me anoon,
For I am out of thi grucching;
I kepe not dele with thee no thing.'
Thus may he shryve hym that forsaketh

His paroch prest, and to me takith;
And if the prest wole hym refuse,
I am full redy hym to accuse,
And hym punysshe and hampre so
That he his chirche shal forgo.
But who so hath in his felyng
The consequence of such shryvyng,
Shall sene that prest may never have
myght
To knowe the conscience a-right
Of hym that is undir his cure.
And this ageyns Holy Scripture,
That biddith every heerde honeste
Have verry knowing of his beeste.
But pore folk that gone by strete,
That have no gold, ne sommes grete,
Hem wolde I lete to her prelates;
Or lete her prestis knowe her states.
Forto me right nought yeve they."

"And why?"
"It is for they ne may.
They ben so bare I take no kepe,
But I wole have the fatte sheepe;
Lat parish prestis have the lene,
I yeve not of her harme a bene,
And if that prelates grucche it,
That oughten wroth be in her witt
To leese her fatte beestes so,
I shal yeve hem a stroke or two
That they shal leesen with [her] force
Ye bothe her mytre and her croce.
Thus jape I hem, and have do longe,
My pryveleges ben so stronge."

Fals-Semblaunt wolde have stynted
heere,
But Love ne made hym no such cheere
That he was wery of his sawe,
But forto make hym glad and fawe
He seide: "Telle on more specialy,
How that thou servest untrewly;
Telle forth, and shame thee never a dele,
For as thyn abit shewith wele
Thou semest an hooly heremyte."
"Sothe is, but I am an ypocrite."
"Thou goste and prechest poverte."
"Ye sir but richesse hath pouste."
"Thou prechest abstinence also."
"Sir, I wole fillen, so mote I go,
My paunche of good mete and [good]
wyne,
As shulde a maister of dyvyne;
For how that I me pover feyne,
Yit all[e] pore folk I disdeyne.
I Love bettir thacqueyntaunce
Ten tyme of the Kyng of Fraunce,
Than of a pore man of mylde mode,
Though that his soule be also gode.
For whanne I see beggers quakyng
Naked on myxnes al stynkyng
For hungre crie, and eke for care,
I entremete not of her fare.
They ben so pore and ful of pyne,
They myght not oonys yeve me a dyne,
For they have no thing but her lyf;
What shulde he yeve that likketh his
knyf?
It is but foly to entremete,
To seke in houndes nest fat mete.
Lete bere hem to the spitel anoon,
But for me comfort gete they noon.

But a riche sike usurere
Wolde I visite and drawe nere;
Hym wole I comforte and rehete,
For I hope of his gold to gete.
And if that wikkid deth hym have,

I wole go with hym to his grave;
And if ther ony reprove me
Why that I lete the pore be,
Wostow how I mot a-scape?
I sey and swere hym ful rape
That riche men han more tecches
Of synne than han pore wrecches,
And han of counsel more mister,
And therfore I wole drawe hem ner.
But as grete hurt, it may so be,
Hath soule in right grete poverte
As soule in grete richesse, forsothe,
Al be it that they hurten bothe;
For richesse and mendicitees
Ben clepid ii. extremytees;
The mene is cleped suffisaunce,
Ther lyth of vertu the aboundaunce.
For Salamon, full wel I wote,
In his Parablis us wrote,
As it is knowe to many a wight,
In his thrittene chapitre right:
'God thou me kepe, for thi pouste,
Fro richesse and mendicite;
For if a riche man hym dresse,
To thenke to myche on [his] richesse,
His herte on that so fer is sett,
That he his creatour foryett;
And hym that begging wole ay greve,
How shulde I bi his word hym leve?
Unnethe [is] that he nys a mycher
Forsworne or ellis God is lyer.'
Thus seith Salamones sawes.
Ne we fynde writen in no lawis
And namely in oure Cristen lay
(Whoso seith, 'Ye,' I dar sey, 'Nay,')
That Crist ne his apostlis dere,
While that they walkide in erthe heere,
Were never seen her bred beggyng;
For they nolde beggen for no thing.
And right thus was men wont to teche,
And in this wise wolde it preche
The maistres of divinite
Somtyme in Parys the citee.
And if men wolde ther-geyn appose
The nakid text and lete the glose,
It myghte soone assoiled be.
For men may wel the sothe see,
That, parde, they myght aske a thing
Pleynly forth without begging;
For they were Goddis herdis deere,
And cure of soules hadden heere.
They nolde no thing begge her fode;
For aftir Crist was done on rode
With ther propre hondis they wrought,
And with travel, and ellis nought,
They wonnen all her sustenaunce,
And lyveden forth in her penaunce,
And the remenaunt yaf awey
To other pore folkis alwey.
They neither bilden tour ne halle,
But ley in houses smale with-alle.
A myghty man that can and may,
Shulde with his honde and body alway,
Wynne hym his fode in laboring,
If he ne have rent or sich a thing,
Al though he be religious,
And god to serven curious.
Thus mote he done, or do trespas,
But if it be in certeyn cas,
That I can reherce if myster be
Right wel, whanne the tyme I se.
Seke the book of seynt Austyne,
Be it in papir or perchemyne,
There as he writ of these worchynges;
Thou shalt seen that noon excusynges
A parfit man ne shulde seke
Bi wordis, ne bi dedis eke,
Al though he be religious

And god to serven curious,
That he ne shal, so mote I go,
With propre hondis and body also,
Gete his fode in laboryng,
If he ne have proprete of thing.
Yit shulde he selle all his substaunce
And with his swynk have sustenaunce,
If he be parfit in bounte;
Thus han tho bookes tolde me.
For he that wole gone ydilly
And usith it ay besily
To haunten other mennes table,
He is a trechour ful of fable,
Ne he ne may by gode resoun
Excuse hym by his orisoun;
For men bihoveth in somme gise
Blynne somtyme in Goddis servise
To gone and purchasen her nede.
Men mote eten, that is no drede,
And slepe, and eke do other thing;
So longe may they leve praiyng;
So may they eke her praier blynne,
While that they werke her mete to wynne.
Seynt Austyn wole therto accorde
In thilke book that I recorde.
Justinian eke, that made lawes,
Hath thus forboden, by old dawes.
No man up peyne to be dede,
Mighty of body, to begge his brede,
If he may swynke it forto gete;
Men shulde hym rather mayme or bete,
Or done of hym aperte justice,
Than suffren hym in such malice.
They done not wel, so mote I go,
That taken such almesse so,
But if they have somme pryvelege,
That of the peyne hem wole allege.
But how that is, can I not see,
But if the prince disseyved be.
Ne I ne wene not sikerly
That they may have it rightfully.
But I wole not determine
Of pryncces power, ne defyne,
Ne by my word comprende, I-wys,
If it so ferre may strecche in this;
I wole not entremete a dele.
But I trowe that the book seith wele,
Who that takith almessis that be
Dewe to folk, that men may se
Lame, feble, wery and bare,
Pore or in such maner care,
That konne wynne hem never mo,
For they have no power therto,
He etith his owne dampnyng,
But if he lye that made al thing.
And if ye such a truaunt fynde,
Chastise hym wel, if ye be kynde.
But they wolde hate you percas,
And if ye fillen in her laas,
They wolde eftsoonys do you scathe,
If that they myghte, late or rathe.
For they be not full pacient,
That han the world thus foule blent.
And witeth wel, that [though] God bad
The good-man selle al that he had,
And folowe hym, and to pore it yive,
He wolde not therfore that he lyve
To serven hym in mendience,
For it was nevere his sentence.
But he bad wirken whanne that neede is,
And folwe hym in goode dedis.
Seynt Poule, that loved al Hooly Chirche,
He bade thappostles forto wirche,
And wynnen her lyflode in that wise,
And hem defended truaundise;
And seide, 'Wirketh with youre honden'
Thus shulde the thing be undirstonden.
He nolde, I-wys, have bidde hem begging.

Ne sellen gospel ne prechyng,
Lest they berafte, with her askyng,
Folk of her catel or of her thing.
For in this world is many a man
That yeveth his good for he ne can
Werne it for shame, or ellis he
Wolde of the asker delyvered be;
And for he hym encombrith so,
He yeveth hym good to late hym go.
But it can hem no thyng profit
They lese the yift and the meryte.
The goode folk that Poule to preched
Profred hym ofte, whan he hem teched,
Somme of her good in charite.
But therfore right no thing toke he,
But of his hondwerk wolde he gete
Clothes to wryne hym, and his mete."

"Telle me thanne how a man may lyven,
That al his good to pore hath yiven,
And wole but oonly bidde his bedis,
And nevere with hondes labour his nede is.
May he do so?"
"Ye sir."
"And how?"

"Sir, I wole gladly telle yow.
Seynt Austyn seith a man may be
In houses that han proprete,
As Templers, and Hospitelers,
And as these Chanouns Regulers,
Or White monkes or these Blake—
I wole no mo ensamplis make—
And take therof his sustenyng,
For therynne lyth no begging;
But other wey[e]s not, y-wys,
Yif Austyn gabbith not of this.
And yit full many a monke laboreth,
That God in hooly chirche honoureth;
For whanne her swynkyng is agone,
They rede and synge in chirche anone.
And for ther hath ben gret discorde,
As many a wight may bere recorde,
Upon the estate of mendience,
I wole shortly, in youre presence,
Telle how a man may begge at nede,
That hath not wherwith hym to fede.
Maugre this felones jangelyngis,
For sothfastnesse wole none hidyngis;
And yit percas I may abey,
That I to yow sothly thus sey.

Lo heere the caas especial:
If a man be so bestial,
That he of no craft hath science,
And nought desireth ignorence,
Thanne may he go a-begging yerne,
Til he somme maner crafte kan lerne;
Thurgh which withoute truaundyng
He may in trouthe have his lyvyng.
Or if he may done no labour
For elde, or sykenesse, or langour,
Or for his tendre age also,
Thanne may he yit a-begging go.
Or if he have peraventure,
Thurgh usage of his norriture,
Lyved over deliciously,
Thanne oughten good folk comunly
Han of his myscheef somme pitee,
And suffren hym also that he
May gone aboute and begge his breed,
That he be not for hungur deed.
Or if he have of craft kunnyng,
And strengthe also, and desiryng
To wirken as he had what
But he fynde neithir this ne that,
Thanne may he begge, til that he
Have geten his necessite.

Or if his wynnyng be so lite
That his labour wole not acquyte
Sufficiantly al his lyvyng,
Yit may he go his breed begging;
Fro dore to dore he may go trace,
Til he the remenaunt may purchace.
Or if a man wolde undirtake
Ony emprise forto make
In the rescous of oure lay,
And it defenden as he may,
Be it with armes or lettrure
Or other covenable cure,
If it be so he pore be,
Thanne may he begge til that he
May fynde in trouthe forto swynke,
And gete hym clothe, mete and drynke,
Swynke he with hondis corporell
And not with hondis espirituell.
In al this caas and in semblables,
If that ther ben mo resonables,
He may begge as I telle you heere,
And ellis nought in no manere;
As William Seynt Amour wolde preche,
And ofte wolde dispute and teche,
Of this mater all openly
At Parys full solempnely.
And, also god my soule blesse,
As he had in this stedfastnesse
The accorde of the universite
And of the puple, as semeth me,
No good man oughte it to refuse,
Ne ought hym therof to excuse.
Be wrothe or blithe who-so be,
For I wole speke and telle it thee,
Al shulde I dye, and be putt doun
As was seynt Poule in derke prisoun,
Or be exiled in this caas
With wrong, as maister William was,
That my moder, Ypocrysie,
Banysshed for hir gret envye.
My modir flemed hym, Seynt Amour:
The noble dide such labour
To susteyne evere the loyalte,
That he to moche agilte me;
He made a book, and lete it write
Wheryn hys lyfe he dyd al write,
And wolde ich reneyed begging,
And lyved by my traveylyng,
If I ne had rent ne other goode.
What! Wened he that I were woode?
For labour myght me never plese,
I have more wille to bene at ese,
And have wel lever, soth to sey,
Bifore the puple patre and prey;
And wrie me in my foxerie
Under a cope of papelardie."
Quod Love, "What devel is this that
I heere?
What wordis tellest thou me heere?"

"What, Sir?"
"Falsnesse that apert is;
Thanne dredist thou not god?"
"No certis;
For selde in grete thing shal he spede
In this worlde, that god wole drede.
For folk that hem to vertu yyven,
And truly on her owne lyven,
And hem in goodnesse ay contene,
On hem is lytel thrift y-sene.
Such folk drinken gret mysese;
That lyf may me never plese.
But se what gold han usurers
And silver eke in [her] garners,
Taylagiers and these monyours,
Bailifs, bedels, provost countours
These lyven wel nygh by ravyne.
The smale puple hem mote enclyne,

And they as wolves wole hem eten.
Upon the pore folk they geten
Full moche of that they spende or kepe.
Nis none of hem that he nyl strepe,
And wrine hem silf wel atte fulle;
Withoute scaldyng they hem pulle.
The stronge the feble overgoth,
But I, that were my symple cloth,
Robbe bothe robbed and robbours,
And gile giled and gilours.
By my treget, I gadre and threste
The gret tresour into my cheste,
That lyth with me so faste bounde.
Myn highe paleys do I founde,
And my delites I fulfille
With wyne at feestes at my wille
And tables full of entremees.
I wole no lyf but ese and pees,
And wynne gold to spende also.
For whanne the grete bagge is go,
It cometh right with my japes.
Make I not wel tumble myn apes?
To wynnen is alwey myn entent,
My purchace is bettir than my rent;
For though I shulde beten be,
Over-al I entremete me;
Withoute me may no wight dure.
I walke soules forto cure,
Of al the worlde cure have I
In brede and lengthe. Bold[e]ly
I wole bothe preche and eke counceilen;
With hondis wille I not traveilen,
For of the Pope I have the bull,
I ne holde not my wittes dull.
I wole not stynten in my lyve
These emperouris forto shryve,
Or kyngis, dukis, lordis grete;
But pore folk al quyte I lete,
I love no such shryvyng, parde;
But it for other cause be,
I rekke not of pore men—
Her astate is not worth an hen;
Where fyndest thou a swynker of labour
Have me unto his confessour?
But emperesses and duchesses,
Thise queenes, and eke countesses,
Thise abbessis, and eke bygyns,
These grete ladyes palasyns,
These joly knyghtis and baillyves,
Thise nonnes, and thise burgeis wyves
That riche ben and eke plesyng,
And thise maidens welfaryng,
Wher so they clad or naked be,
Uncounceiled goth ther noon fro me.
And for her soules savete
At lord and lady and her meyne
I axe, whanne thei hem to me shryve,
The proprete of al her lyve,
And make hem trowe, bothe meest
and leest,
Hir paroch prest nys but a beest
Ayens me and my companye,
That shrewis ben as gret as I.
Fro whiche I wole not hide in holde
No pryvete that me is tolde,
That I, by word or signe y-wis,
[Nyl] make hem knowe what it is.
And they wolen also tellen me,
They hele fro me no pryvyte,
And forto make yow hem perceyven,
That usen folk thus to disceyven,
I wole you seyn withouten drede
What men may in the gospel rede
Of seynt Mathew, the gospelere,
That seith as I shal you sey heere:

'Uppon the chaire of Moyses
(Thus is it glosed douteles:

That is the Olde Testament,
For ther-by is the chaire ment)
Sitte Scribes and Pharisen
(That is to seyn, the cursid men
Whiche that we ypocritis calle).
Doth that they preche, I rede you alle,
But doth not as they don a dele;
That ben not wery to seye wele,
But to do wel no will have they.
And they wolde bynde on folk al-wey,
That ben to be giled able,
Burdons that ben importable.
On folkes shuldris thinges they couchen,
That they nyl with her fyngris touchen.'

"And why wole they not touche it?"
"Why,
For hem ne lyst not sikirly,
For sadde burdons that men taken,
Make folkes shuldris aken.
And if they do ought that good be,
That is for folk it shulde se.
Her bordurs larger maken they,
And make her hemmes wide alwey,
And loven setes at the table,
The firste and moste honourable,
And forto han the firste chaieris
In synagogis to hem full deere is,
And willen that folk hem loute and grete,
Whanne that they passen thurgh the strete,
And wolen be cleped 'Maister' also.
But they ne shulde not willen so,
The gospel is ther-ageyns, I gesse,
That shewith wel her wikkidnesse.

Another custome use we
Of hem that wole ayens us be;
We hate hym deedly everichone,
And we wole werrey hym as oon;
Hym that oon hatith hate we alle,
And congecte how to done hym falle.
And if we seen hym wynne honour,
Richesse, or preis, thurgh his valour,
Provende, rent, or dignyte,
Full fast y-wys compassen we
Bi what ladder he is clomben so;
And forto maken hym doun to go
With traisoun we wole hym defame,
And done hym leese his goode name.
Thus from his ladder we hym take,
And thus his freendis foes we make.
But word ne wite shal he noon,
Till all hise freendis ben his foon.
For if we dide it openly
We myght have blame redily;
For hadde he wist of oure malice,
He hadde hym kept, but he were nyce.

Another is this, that if so falle
That ther be oon amonge us alle
That doth a good turne out of drede,
We seyn it is oure alder deede.
Ye sikerly though he it feyned,
Or that hym list, or that hym deyned
A man thurgh hym avaunced be,
Therof all parseners be we,
And tellen folk where so we go,
That man thurgh us is sprongen so.
And forto have of men preysyng,
We purchace thurgh oure flateryng
Of riche men of gret pouste
Lettres to witnesse oure bounte,
So that man weneth that may us see
That alle vertu in us be.
And al-wey pore we us feyne;
But how so that we begge or pleyne,
We ben the folk without lesyng
That all thing have without havyng.
Thus be we dred of the puple y-wis.

And gladly my purpos is this:
I dele with no wight but he
Have gold and tresour gret plente;
Her acqueyntaunce wel love I,
This is moche my desire shortly.
I entremete me of brokages,
I make pees and mariages,
I am gladly executour,
And many tymes procuratour;
I am somtyme messager
(That fallith not to my myster),
And many tymes I make enquestes—
For me that office not honest is.
To dele with other mennes thing,
That is to me a gret lykyng.
And if that ye have ought to do
In place that I repeire to,
I shal it speden thurgh my witt,
As soone as ye have told me it.
So that ye serve me to pay,
My servyse shal be youre alway;
But who-so wole chastise me,
Anoon my love lost hath he.
For I love no man in no gise
That wole me repreve or chastise;
But I wolde al folk undirtake,
And of no wight no teching take;
For I that other folk chastie,
Wole not be taught fro my folie.
I love noon hermitage more;
All desertes, and holtes hore,
And grete wodes everichon,
I lete hem to the Baptist Iohn.
I quethe hym quyte, and hym relese
Of Egipt all the wildirnesse.
To ferre were alle my mansiouns
Fro al citees and goode tounes;
My paleis and myn hous make I
There men may renne ynne openly;
And sey that I the world forsake,
But al amydde I bilde and mak
My hous, and swimme and pley therynne,
Bet than a fish doth with his fynne.
Of Antecristes men am I,
Of whiche that Crist seith openly,
They have abit of hoolynesse,
And lyven in such wikkednesse.
Outward lambren semen we,
Full of goodnesse and of pitee,
And inward we withouten fable
Ben gredy wolves ravysable.
We enviroune bothe londe and se,
With all the worlde werrien we;
We wole ordeyne of alle thing,
Of folkis good and her lyvyng.
If ther be castel or citee
Wherynne that ony bourgerons be,
Al though that they of Milayne were
(For therof ben they blamed there);
Or if a wight out of mesure
Wolde lene his gold and take usure,
For that he is so coveitous;
Or if he be to leccherous,
Or these that haunte symonye,
Or provost full of trecherie,
Or prelat lyvyng jolily,
Or prest that halt his quene hym by,
Or olde horis hostilers,
Or other bawdes or bordillers,
Or elles blamed of ony vice
Of whiche men shulden done justice:
Bi all the seyntes that me pray,
But they defende them with lamprey,
With luce, with elys, with samons,
With tendre gees, and with capons,
With tartes, or with chesis fat,
With deynte flawns brode and flat,
With caleweis, or with pullaylle,

With conynges, or with fyne vitaille,
That we undir our clothes wide
Maken thourgh oure golet glide,
Or but he wole do come in haste
Roo-venysoun bake in paste,
Whether so that he loure or groyne,
He shal have of a corde a loigne
With whiche men shal hym bynde
and lede
To brenne hym for his synful deede,
That men shull here hym crie and rore,
A myle-wey aboute and more;
Or ellis he shal in prisoun dye,
But if he wole his frendship bye,
Or smerten that that he hath do
More than his gilt amounteth to.
But and he couthe thurgh his sleight
Do maken up a tour of height,—
Nought rought I whethir of stone, or tree,
Or erthe or turves though it be,
Though it were of no vounde stone
Wrought with squyre and scantilone,
So that the tour were stuffed well
With alle richesse temporell—
And thanne that he wolde updresse
Engyns bothe more and lesse,
To cast at us by every side
To bere his goode name wide,
Such flightes [as] I shal yow nevene,
Barelles of wyne by sixe or sevene
Or gold in sakkis gret plente,
He shulde soone delyvered be.
And if he have noon sich pitaunces,
Late hym study in equipolences,
And late lyes and fallaces,
If that he wolde deserve oure graces;
Or we shal bere hym such witnesse
Of synne and of his wrecchidnesse,
And done his loos so wide renne,
That al quyk we shulden hym brenne,
Or ellis yeve hym suche penaunce
That is wel wors than the pitaunce.
For thou shalt never for no thing
Kon knowen a-right by her clothing
The traitours full of trecherie,
But thou her werkis can a-spie.
And ne hadde the good kepyng be
Whilom of the universite
That kepith the key of Cristendome
We had bene turmented, al and some.
Suche ben the stynkyng prophetis;
Nys none of hem that good prophete is,
For they thurgh wikked entencioun,
The yeer of the Incarnacioun
A thousand and two hundred yeer,
Fyve and fifty, ferther ne ner,
Broughten a book with sory grace
To yeven ensample in comune place,
That seide thus though it were fable:
'This is the Gospel Perdurable,
That fro the Holy Goost is sent.'—
Wel were it worthi to bene brent!
Entitled was in such manere
This book, of which I telle heere
Ther nas no wight in all Parys
Biforne Oure Lady at parvys
That he ne mighte bye the book
To copy, if hym talent toke.
There myght he se by gret tresoun
Full many fals comparisoun:—
'As moche as thurgh his gret myght,
Be it of hete or of lyght,
The sonne sourmounteth the mone,
That trouble is and chaungith soone,
And the note kernell the shell—
(I scorne not, that I yow tell)—
Right so, withouten ony gile,
Sourmounteth this noble Evangile

The word of ony evangelist.'
And to her title they token Crist.
And many such comparisoun
Of which I make no mencioun,
Mighte men in that book fynde
Who so coude of hem have mynde.

The Universite, that tho was a-slepe,
Gan forto braide and taken kepe,
And at the noys the heed upcast,
Ne never sithen slept it fast;
But up it stert, and armes toke
Ayens this false horrible boke,
Al redy bateil for to make,
And to the juge the book to take.
But they that broughten the boke there
Hent it anoon awey for fere;
They nolde shewe more a dele
But thenne it kept, and kepen will,
Til such a tyme that they may see
That they so stronge woxen be,
That no wyght may hem wel withstonde.
For by that book they durst not stonde.
Awey they gonne it forto bere,
For they ne durste not answere
By exposicioun ne glose
To that that clerkis wole appose
Ayens the cursednesse y-wys
That in that booke writen is.
Now wote I not, ne I can not see
What maner eende that there shal be
Of al this [bokes] that they hyde;
But yit algate they shal abide
Til that they may it bet defende,
This trowe I best wole be her ende.
Thus Antecrist abiden we,
For we ben alle of his meyne;
And what man that wole not be so,
Right soone he shal his lyf forgo.
We wole a puple upon hym areyse,
And thurgh oure gile done hym seise,
And hym on sharpe speris ryve,
Or other weyes brynge hym fro lyve,
But if that he wole folowe y-wis
That in oure booke writen is.
Thus mych wole oure book signifie,
That while Petre hath maistrie,
May never Iohn shewe well his myght.
Now have I you declared right
The menyng of the bark and rynde,
That makith the entenciouns blynde;
But now at erst I wole bigynne,
To expowne you the pith withynne:—

. . . .

And the seculers comprehende,
That Cristes lawe wole defende,
And shulde it kepen and mayntenen
Ayenes hem that all sustenen,
And falsly to the puple techen.
That Iohn bitokeneth hem that prechen
That ther nys lawe covenable
But thilke Gospel Perdurable,
That fro the Holygost was sent
To turne folk that ben myswent.
The strengthe of Iohn, they undirstonde
The grace in which they seie they stonde,
That doth the synfull folk converte
And hem to Iesus Crist reverte.
Full many another orriblite
May men in that booke se,
That ben comaunded douteles
Ayens the lawe of Rome expres;
And all with Antecrist they holden,
As men may in the book biholden.
And thanne comaunden they to sleen
Alle tho that with Petre been;
But they shal nevere have that myght,
And God to-forne for strif to fight,

That they ne shal enowe fynde,
That Petres lawe shal have in mynde,
And evere holde, and so mayntene;
That at the last it shal be sene
That they shal alle come therto
For ought that they can speke or do.
And thilke lawe shal not stonde
That they by Iohn have undirstonde,
But, maugre hem, it shal adowne,
And bene brought to confusioun.

But I wole stynt of this matere,
For it is wonder longe to here.
But hadde that ilke book endured,
Of better estate I were ensured;
And freendis have I yit pardee
That han me sett in gret degre.
Of all this world is Emperour
Gyle my fadir, the trechour,
And Emperis my moder is,
Maugre the Holygost y-wis.
Oure myghty lynage and oure rowte
Regneth in every regne aboute.
And well is worthy we [maystres] be;
For all this world governe we,
And can the folk so wel disceyve,
That noon oure gile can perceyve;
And though they done, they dar not sey,
The sothe dar no wight bywray.
But he in Cristis wrath hym ledith
That more than Crist my britheren dredith.
He nys no full good champioun
That dredith such similacioun,
Nor that for peyne wole refusen
Us to correcte and accusen.
He wole not entremete by right,
Ne have God in his eye-sight;
And therfore God shal hym punyce.
But me ne rekketh of no vice,
Sithen men us loven comunably,
And holden us for so worthy,
That we may folk repreve echoon,
And we nyl have repref of noon.
Whom shulden folk worshipen so
But us, that stynten never mo
To patren while that folk may us see,
Though it not so bihynde hem be.
And where is more wode folye
Than to enhaunce chyvalrie,
And love noble men and gay,
That joly clothis weren alway?
If they be sich folk as they semen,
So clene as men her clothis demen,
And that her wordis folowe her dede,
It is gret pite, out of drede,
For they wole be noon ypocritis!
Of hem me thynketh [it] gret spite is;
I can not love hem on no side.
But beggers with these hodes wide,
With sleigh and pale faces lene,
And greye clothis not full clene,
But fretted full of tatarwagges,
And highe shoes knopped with dagges,
That frouncen lyke a quaile-pipe,
Or botis revelyng as a gype;
To such folk as I you dyvyse
Shulde princes and these lordis wise
Take all her londis and her thingis,
Bothe werre and pees in governyngis;
To such folk shulde a prince hym yive,
That wolde his lyf in honour lyve.
And if they be not as they seme,
That serven thus the world to queme,
There wolde I dwelle to disceyve
The folk, for they shal not perceyve.
But I ne speke in no such wise
That men shulde humble abit dispise,

So that no pride ther-undir be.
No man shulde hate, as thynkith me,
The pore man in sich clothyng.
But God ne preisith hym no thing
That seith he hath the world forsake,
And hath to worldly glorie hym take,
And wole of siche delices use.
Who may that begger wel excuse,
That papelard that hym yeldith so,
And wole to worldly ese go,
And seith that he the world hath lefte,
And gredily it grypeth efte ?
He is the hounde, shame is to seyn,
That to his castyng goth ageyn.
But unto you dar I not lye ;
But myght I felen or aspie
That ye perceyved it no thyng,
Ye shulde have a stark lesyng
Right in youre honde thus, to bigynne,
I nolde it lette ror no synne."

The god lough at the wondir tho,
And every wight gan laugh also,
And seide :—" Lo heere a man, a right
Forto be trusty to every wight ! "

"Falssemblant," quod Love, " sey to me,
Sith I thus have advaunced thee
That in my court is thi dwellyng,
And of ribawdis shalt be my kyng,
Wolt thou wel holden my forwardis ? "
"Yhe, sir, from hennes forewardis ;
Hadde never youre fadir heere biforne
Servaunt so trewe, sith he was borne."

" That is ageynes all nature."

" Sir, putte you in that aventure ;
For though ye borowes take of me,
The sikerer shal ye never be
For ostages, ne sikirnsese,
Or chartres, forto bere witnesse
I take youre silf to recorde heere,
That men ne may, in no manere,
Teren the wolf out of his hide,
Til he be flayen bak and side,
Though men hym bete and al defile.
What ! Wene ye that I wole bigile ?
For I am clothed mekely,
Ther-undir is all my trechery ;
Myn herte chaungith never the mo
For noon abit in which I go.
Though I have chere of symplenesse,
I am not wery of shrewidnesse.
Myn lemman Streyneth-Abstinence,
Hath myster of my purveaunce ;
She hadde ful longe ago be deede,
Nere my councel and my rede ;
Lete hir allone and you and me."

And Love answerde : " I truste thee
Withoute borowe for I wole noon."

And Falssemblant, the theef, anoon
Ryght in that ilke same place,
That hadde of tresoun al his face
Ryght black withynneand white without,
Thankyth hym, ganon his knees loute.

Thanne was ther nought but " Every man
Now to assaut that sailen can,"
Quod Love, "and that full hardyly !"
Thanne armed they hem communly
Of sich armour as to hem felle.
Whanne the were armed fers and felle,
They wente hem forth all in a route,

And set the castel al aboute.
They will nought away for no drede,
Till it so be that they ben dede,
Or till they have the castel take.
And foure batels they gan make,
And parted hem in foure anoon,
And toke her way and forth they gone,
The foure gates forto assaile,
Of whiche the kepers wole not faile.
For they ben neithir sike ne dede,
But hardy folk and stronge in dede.

Now wole I seyn the countynaunce
Of Falssemblant and Abstynaunce,
That ben to Wikkid-Tonge went.
But first they heelde her parlement
Whether it to done were
To maken hem be knowen there,
Or elles walken forth disgised.
But at the laste they devysed
That they wolde gone in tapinage,
As it were in a pilgrimage,
Lyke good and hooly folk unfeyned.
And Dame Abstinence-Streyned
Toke on a robe of kamelyne,
And gan hir graithe as a Bygynne.
A large coverechief of threde
She wrapped all aboute hir heede ;
But she forgate not hir sawter;
A peire of bedis eke she bere
Upon a lace all of white threde,
On which that she hir bedes bede.
But she ne bought hem never a dele,
For they were geven her I wote wele,
God wote, of a full hooly frere,
That seide he was hir fadir dere
To whom she hadde ofter went
Than ony frere of his covent.
And he visited hir also,
And many a sermoun seide hir to ;
He nolde lette for man on lyve
That he ne wolde hir ofte shryve,
And with so great devocion
They made her confession,
That they had ofte, for the nones,
Two heedes in one hoode at ones.

Of fayre shappe I devyse her the,
But pale of face somtyme was she;
That false traytouresse untrewe,
Was lyke that salowe horse of hewe,
That in the Apocalips is shewed,
That signifyeth tho folke beshrewed,
That ben al ful of trecherye
And pale through hypocrisye.
For on that horse no colour is,
But onely deed and pale y-wis,
Of suche a colour enlangoured
Was Abstynence i-wys coloured;
Of her estate she her repented,
As her visage represented.

She had a burdowne al of Thefte,
That Gyle had yeve her of his yefte;
And a skryppe of Faynte Distresse,
That ful was of elengenesse.
And forthe she walked sobrely;
And False Semblant saynt *je vous die*,
Had, as it were for suche mistere,
Done on the cope of a frere.
With chere symple and ful pytous,
Hys lokyng was not disdeynous
Ne proude, but meke and ful pesyble.

About his neck he bare a byble,
And squierly forthe gan he gon;
And, for to rest his lymmes upon,
He had of Treson a potent;

As he were feble his way he went.
But in his sleve he gan to thring
A rasour sharpe, and wel bytyng,
That was forged in a forge,
Whichethat men clepen Coupe-gorge.
So longe forthe her waye they nomen,
Tyl they to Wicked-Tonge comen.
That at his gate was syttyng,
And sawe folke in the way passyng.
The pilgrymes sawe he faste by,
That beren hem ful mekely,
And humbly they with him mette,
Dame Abstynence first him grette,
And sythe him False-Semblant salued,
And he hem; but he not remeued
For he ne dredde hem not a dele.
For whan he sawe her faces wele,
Alway in herte hem thought so,
He shulde knowe hem bothe two;
For wel heknewe Dame Abstynaunce,
But he ne knewe not Constreynaunce.
He knewenat thatshe wasconstrayned,
Ne of her theves lyfe [y-]fayned,
But wende she come of wyl al free;
But she come in another degree;
And if of good wyl she beganne
That wyl was fayled her [as] thanne.
And False-Semblant had he sayne alse,
But he knewe nat that he was false.
Yet false was he, but his falsnesse
Ne coude he nat espye nor gesse;
For Semblant was so slye wrought,
That Falsenesse he ne espyed nought.

But haddest thou knowen hym beforne
Thou woldest on a boke have sworne,
Whan thou him saugh in thylke araye,
That he that whilome was so gaye,
And of the daunce joly Robyn,
Was tho become a Iacobyn.
But sothely what so menne hym calle,
Freres Prechours bene good menne alle,
Her order wickedly they beren,
Suche myn[e]strelles if they weren.

So bene Augustyns and Cordyleres
And Carmes, and eke Sacked freeres
And alle freres, shodde and bare,
(Though some of hem ben gret and square)
Ful hooly men, as I hem deme.
Everycheofhem woldegoodmanseme;
But shalte thou never of apparence
Sene conclude good consequence
In none argument y-wis
If existens al fayled is.
Formennemayefynde alwayesophyme
The consequence to envenyme,
Who so that hath hadde the subtelte
The double sentence for to se.

Whan the pylgrymes commen were
To Wicked-Tonge that dwelled there,
Her harneys nygh hem was algate;
By Wicked-Tonge adowne they sate,
That badde hem nere him for to come
And of tidynges telle him some,
Andsaydhem: "Whatcasemaketh you
To come in-to this place nowe?"

"Sir," sayd Strayned-Abstynaunce,
"We, for to drye our penaunce
With hertes pytous and devoute
Are commen,as pylgrimes gon aboute:
Wel nygh on fote always we go;
Ful dousty ben our heeles two.
And thus bothe we ben sent

Throughout this worlde that is miswent,
To yeve ensample, and preche also.
To fysshen synful menne we go,
For other fysshynge, ne fysshe we.
And, sir, for that charyte,
As we be wonte, herborowe we crave
Your lyfe to amende, Christ it save,
And so it shulde you nat displese,
We wolden, if it were your ese,
A shorte sermon unto you sayne."
And Wicked-Tonge answered agayne:

"The house," quod he, "such as ye se
Shal nat be warned you for me,
Say what you lyst, and I wol here."

"Graunt mercy, swete sir, dere,"
Quod alderfirst Dame Abstynence,
And thus began she her sentence:

"Sir, the firste vertue certayne,
The greatest, and moste soverayne
That may be founde in any man
For havynge or for wytte he can,
That is his tonge to refrayne.
Therto ought every wight him payne,
For it is better stylle be
Than for to speken harme, parde;
And he that herkeneth it gladly,
He is no good man sykerly.

And, sir, aboven al other synne,
In that arte thou moste gylty inne.
Thou spake a jape not long a-go
(And, sir, that was ryght yvel do)
Of a yonge man, that here repayred
And never yet this place apayred.
Thou saydest he awayted nothyng
But to disceyve Fayre-Welcomyng.
Ye sayde nothyng sothe of that;
But, sir, ye lye, I tel you plat;
He ne cometh no more, ne gothe, parde!
I trowe ye shal him never se.
Fayre-Welcomyng in prison is,
That ofte hath played with you er this
The fayrest games that he coude,
Withoute fylthe, styl or loude;
Nowe dare he nat him selfe solace.
Ye han also the manne do chace,
That he dare neyther come ne go;
What meveth you to hate him so,
But properly your wicked thought,
That many a false lesyng hath thought,
That meveth your foole eloquence,
That jangleth ever in audyence,
And on the folke areyseth blame,
And doth hem dishonour and shame,
For thynge that maye have no prevyng
But lykelynesse, and contryvyng?

For I dare sayne that reason demeth,
It is nat al sothe thynge that semeth;
And it is synne to controve
Thynge that is to reprove;
This wote ye wele; and, sir, therfore
Ye arne to blame [wel] the more.
And nathelesse he recketh lyte
He yeveth nat nowe therof a myte,
For if he thoughte harme, parfaye,
He wolde come and gone al daye;
He coude himselfe nat abstene.
Now cometh he nat, and that is sene,
For he ne taketh of it no cure,
But if it be through aventure,
And lasse than other folke, algate.
And thou her watchest at the gate,
With speare in thyne arest alwaye;
There muse, musarde, al the daye.

Thou wakest night and day for thought;
I-wis thy traveyle is for nought.
And Ielousye, withouten fayle,
Shal never quyte the thy traveyle.
And skathe is that Fayre-Welcomyng
Withouten any trespassyng,
Shal wrongfully in prison be,
There wepeth and languyssheth he.
And though thou never yet, y-wis,
Agyltest manne no more but this,—
Take nat a grefe,—it were worthy
To putte the out of this bayly,
And afterwards in prison lye,
And fettre the, tyl that thou dye.
For thou shalt for this synne dwelle
Right in the devels ers of helle,
But if that thou repente thee."
"Mafay, thou liest falsly!" quod he.
"What? welcome with myschaunce nowe!
Have I therfore herberd yowe
To seye me shame, and eke reprove
With sory happe, to youre bihove?
Am I to day youre herbegere?
Go herber yow elles-where than heere,
That han a lyer called me!
Two tregetours art thou and he,
That in myn hous do me this shame,
And for my sothe-saugh ye me blame.
Is this the sermoun that ye make?
To all the develles I me take,
Or elles, God, thou me confounde!
But er men diden this castel founde,
It passith not ten daies or twelve
But it was tolde right to my selve,
And as they seide, right so tolde I:
He kyst the Rose pryvyly!
Thus seide I now and have seid yore;
I not where he dide ony more.
Why shulde men sey me such a thyng
If it hadde bene gabbyng?
Ryght so seide I and wol seye yit;
I trowe I lied not of it.
And with my bemes I wole blowe
To alle neighboris a-rowe,
How he hath bothe comen and gone."
Tho spake Falssemblant right anone:
"All is not gospel, oute of doute,
That men seyn in the towne aboute;
Ley no deef ere to my spekyng;
I swere yow, sir, it is gabbyng;
I trowe ye wote wel certeynly,
That no man loveth hym tenderly
That seith hym harme, if he wote it,
All be he never so pore of wit.
And soth is also sikerly
(This knowe ye, sir, as wel as I)
That lovers gladly wole visiten
The places there her loves habiten.
This man yow loveth and eke honoureth
This man to serve you laboureth,
And clepith you 'his freend so deere,'
And this man makith you good chere,
And every-where that [he] you meteth
He yow saloweth and he you greteth.
He preseth not so ofte that ye
Ought of his come encombred be;
Ther presen other folk on yow
Full ofter than he doth now.
And if his herte hym streyned so,
Unto the Rose forto go,
Ye shulde hym sene so ofte nede,
That ye shulde take hym with the dede.
He cowde his comyng not forbere
Though he hym thrilled with a spere;
It nere not thanne as it is now.
But trustith wel, I swere it yow,
That it is clene out of his thought;

Sir, certis he ne thenkith it nought,
No more ne doth Faire-Welcomyng,
That sore abieth al this thing.
And if they were of oon assent,
Full soone were the Rose hent,
The maugre youres wolde be.
And, sir, of o thing herkeneth me:
Sith ye this man that loveth yow
Han seid such harme and shame now,
Witeth wel if he gessed it,
Ye may wel demen in youre wit
He nolde no thyng love you so,
Ne callen you his freende also;
But nyght and day he wolde wake
The castell to destroie and take,
If it were soth as ye devise;
Or some man in some maner wise,
Might it warne hym everydele,
Or by hymsilf perceyven wele.
For sith he myght not come and gone
As he was whilom wont to done,
He myght it sone wite and see.
But now all other wise doth he.
Thanne have, [ye] sir, al outerly
Deserved helle, and Iolyly
The deth of helle douteles,
That thrallen folk so gilteles."

Fals Semblant proveth so this thing,
That he can noon answeryng,
And seth alwey such apparaunce,
That nygh he fel in repentaunce
And seide hym:—"Sir, it may wel be,
Semblant, a good man semen ye;
And, Abstinence, full wise ye seme;
Of o talent you bothe I deme.
What counceil wole ye to me yeven?"
"Ryghtheereanoon thoushaltbeshryven
And sey thy synne withoute more;
Of this shalt thou repente sore.
For I am prest, and have pouste
To shryve folk of most dignyte
That ben, as wide as world may dure,
Of all this world I have the cure,
And that hadde never yit persoun,
Ne vicarie of no maner toun.
And, God wote, I have of thee
A thousand tyme more pitee
Than hath thi preest parochial,
Though he thy freend be special.
I have avauntage in o wise
That youre prelatis ben not so wise,
Ne half so lettred as am I.
I am licenced boldely
To rede in Divinite
And to confessen, out of drede.
If ye wol you now confesse,
And leve your sinnes more and lesse
Withoute abood, knele down anon,
And you shal have absolucion."

THE END

Semblant, a good man semen ye;
And, Abstinence, full wise ye seme;
Of o talent you bothe I deme.
What counceil wole ye to me yeven?"
"Ryght heere anoon thou shalt be shryve
And sey thy synne withoute more;
Of this shalt thou repente sore.
For I am prest, and have pouste
To shryve folk of most dignyte
That ben, as wide as world may dure,
Of all this world I have the cure,
And that hadde never yit persoun,
Ne vicarie of no maner toun.
And, God wote, I have of thee
A thousand tyme more pitee
Than hath thi preest parochial,
Though he thy freend be special.
I have avauntage in o wise
That youre prelatis ben not so wise,
Ne half so lettred as am I.
I am licenced boldely
To rede in Divinite
And to confessen, out of drede.
If ye wol you now confesse,
And leve your sinnes more and lesse
Withoute abood, knele down anon,
And you shal have absolucion."

HERE ENDS THE ROMAUNT OF THE ROSE IN THE VERSION ASCRIBED TO GEOFFREY CHAUCER. BY COURTEOUS PERMISSION OF MESSRS MACMILLAN & CO, THE TEXT FOLLOWED IS THAT EDITED BY PROF. MARK H. LIDDELL IN THE GLOBE EDITION

GLOSSARY

ABIETH, pays for
ABOOD, delay
ABRAIDE, ABREYD, awoke
ACOYE, coax
ADAMAUND, magnet
AFFRAIETH, arouses
AFFYE, trust
AGULER, needle-case
AGYLTE, offend
ALDER, of all
ALDERFIRST, first of all
ALEYS, fruit of the service-tree
ALGATE, any way
ALOSED, praised
ALPES, bullfinches
ALTO-SHARE, cut in pieces
APAIED, contented
APPERT, open
ARCHAUNGELL, titmouse
AREST, in rest
ATTEMPRE, temperate
AUNTRE, adventure
AVAUNT, forward
AVENAUNT, comely
AVYSION, vision
AWMERE, bag for alms

BAALIS BEETE, bale's boot—harm's cure
BAUDE, gay
BAUNDON, power
BERNE, barn
BESAUNT, a small gold coin
BESAUNT-WIGHT, the weight of a besaunt
BIGOO, clothed
BIMENE, bemoan
BISEKE, beseech
BISETT, employs
BLENT, to blench
BLYNNE, cease
BOLAS, bullace, the wild plum
BORDILLERS, brothel-keepers
BOROWES, pledges
BRAIDE, start
BURNET COTE, brown garment
BURNETTES, brown garments
BYGYNS, béguines, a charitable order of women
BYHOTE, promise
BYNOMEN, taken away
BYRDE, bride
BYSTADDE, bestead
BYTRASSHED, betrayed

CALEWEIS, pears
CANELL, cinnamon
CHELAUNDRE, lark
CHEVESAILE, collar
CHEVISAUNCE, bargain
CHICHE, CHYNCHY, niggardly
CIERGIS, tapers
CLAPERS, burrows
CLOWE-GELOFRE, clove-gillyflower
COMYN, common
CONTROVE, contrive
CONYNGES, rabbits
CORDE A LOIGNE, tether-cord
CORDYLERES, a Franciscan order
CORUMPABLE, corruptible
COSSE, kiss
COUNTOURS, auditors
COURTEPY, short cloak
COVENABLE, fit
COVYNE, deceit
CRIANDE, crying
CUNNE, study

DAMPNYNG, condemning
DAUNGERE, power, or domain
DAWES, days
DECOPED, slit
DELICES, delights
DELYVER, quick
DELYVERLY, nimbly
DEVER, duty
DEYNOUS, DEIGHNOUS, disdainful
DISPITOUS, contemptuous
DOANDE, doing
DOME, judgment
DRUERIE, affection
DURST, need

EGRE, sharp
EISEL, vinegar
ELENGENESSE, misery
EMPRISE, enterprise
ENCHESOUN, occasion
ENTREMETE, interfere
EQUIPOLENCES, equivalents
ERKE, weary
ERNES, pledges
ESTERS, ESTRES, ESTREES, inmost part of a house

FARCE, paint
FAWE, fain
FELE, many
FETTE, fetched
FETYS, neat
FLAWNS, pancakes
FLEMED, exiled
FLOWTOURS, pipers
FOISOUN, increase
FONDE, foolishly
FORDWYNED, wasted
FORPYNED, wretched
FORTHENKE, repent
FORWELKED, withered
FORWERED, worn out
FOR-WO, weary
FRETT, adorned
FROUNCED, wrinkled

GADELYNG, vagabond
GNEDE, gnawed
GOLET, gullet
GOUNFANOUN, banner
GRAITHE, GRAYTHE, prepare
GREE (TAKE ATTE), agree to
GREVE, grove
GREYN DE PARADYS, a kind of spice
GROYNE, grant
GRUCCHING, grumbling
GYPE, tunic
GYSARME, halberd

HAIRE, hair-shirt
HATTE, be called
HAWTEYNE, haughty
HAYE, hedge
HEERDIS, coarse flax
HENDE, gracious
HENT, caught
HERBEJOURS, harbingers
HOLSTRED, concealed
HONDE, hand
HOOLE, whole
HORIS, prostitutes
HOTE, promise
HOTETH, promises

JAGOUNCES, jacinths
JANGELYNGIS, chatterings
JUPARTIE, jeopardy

KAMELYNE, camel's hair
KAROLE, a dance, singing
KEPE, care
KERNELS, loopholes
KIDDE, revealed
KIRKED, crooked
KNOPPIS, buds

LAAS, snare
LACCHE, snare
LAVEROKKES, larks
LEMES, beams
LENYNG, lending
LEPANDE, leaping
LERE, learn
LESYNGES, falsehoods
LETTRURE, learning
LOIGNE, tether
LOOS, fame
LORERES, bay-trees
LOSENGERE, flatterer
LOTEBY, paramour
LOURE, lower
LOWITH, praises

MAATE, dejected
MANGONEL, a military engine
MAUGREE, in spite of
MENTES, mint
MES, advantage
MEVERESSE, agitator
MEYGNED, maimed
MEYNDE, mingled
MOEBLE, movable
MOURDAUNT, part of the girdle
MOWE, may
MOWIS, stacks or heaps in a barn
MOYSOUN, crop

GLOSSARY

MUSARDE, dreamer
MYCHER, thief
MYSSEYE, traduce
MYSSAIERE, scandal-monger
MYSTER, need

NEDELY, of necessity
NEIGH, nigh, come nigh
NEMPNED, called
NOKKED, notched
NORRITURE, nurture
NYCETE, folly

OLMERIS, elms
OMAGER, vassal
ONDE, hatred
ORFRAYS, embroidery in gold

PAIE, content
PALASIE, palsy
PALASYNS, palaces
PAPELARDIE, deceit
PARSENERS, partners
PATRE, to repeat prayers
PEIRE, injure
PENSEL, banner
PERDURABLE, enduring
PERELL, pearl
PERSANT, piercing
POPPED, over-dressed
POSSED, pushed
POTENT (BY), with a crutch
POUSTE, power
POYNTEN, prick or probe
POYNT DEVYS (AT), minutely
PRECE, press
PREY, pray
PRILLE, spin round
PROVENDE, food
PROWE, profit
PULLAYLLE, fowl
PUPLE, people
PURVEAUNCE, providence
PYMENT, spiced wine and honey

QUARELS, cross-bow bolts
QUEME, please
QUOINT, quaint
QUYSTROUN, scullion

RACYNE, root
RAMAGE, wild
RAPE, haste
RECCHITH, care
REFUYT, refuge
REHETE, cheer
REMEUED, removed
RESCOUS, rescue
REVED, robbed
RISHE, rush
ROKET, linen vest
RONE, bush
ROUKYNG, cowering
ROYNE, scurf
RYVE, pierce

SAILLOURIS, dancers
SAUFF, except
SCANTILONE, mason's rule
SCOCHOUNS, escutcheons
SETEWALE, valerian
SHENDE, harm
SHENDITH, confounds
SHERE, shorn
SHOF, shoved
SIBBE, related
SIKERLY, surely
SITTANDE, fitting
SKATHE, harm
SLOWE, sluggard
SOTHE-SAWE, true story
SOUPLE, pliant
SOUPLEN, make pliant
SPARTHE, axe
SPAUNYSSHINGE, blooming
SPRYNGOLDES, stone-throwers
STARFE, died
STONTE, stand
STOUNDE-MELE, at times
STOUNDES, instants
STYF IN STOUR, stubborn in conflict
SUKKENYE, a jacket
SWEVENINGES, dreams
SWIRE, throat
SWITHE, quickly

TAPINAGE, hiding
TATARWAGGES, tatters
TEMPRURE, tempering
TENE, sorrow

GLOSSARY

TERINS, finches
THWYTEN, whittled
TO-DRAWE, to draw asunder
TO-SLYTERED, slashed
TREGET, trickery
TREPEGET, engine for casting stones
TRETYS, well-formed
TROWANDYSE, TRUANDISE, vagrancy
TWYNNE, separate
TYMBRES, timbrels or tabors
TYMBESTER, a timbrel-player

UNNETHE, scarcely

VEER YLICHE, spring-like
VEKKE, old woman
VOLAGE, giddy

WARISOUN, reward
WARNEN, denied
WEM, blemish
WENE, doubt
WERE, danger
WERNE, refuse
WERREID, persecuted
WEYMENTYNG, lamentation
WISLY, surely
WODEWALES, a kind of bird
WOLL, wool, will
WONE, abundance
WOODE, mad
WREYING, betrayal
WRINE, WRYNE, cover
WYNDRE, to trim the hair

YEECHYNG, itching
YERNE, desirous
YFERE, together
YMPED, grafted
YNDE, indigo

Printed by BALLANTYNE, HANSON & Co.
Edinburgh & London

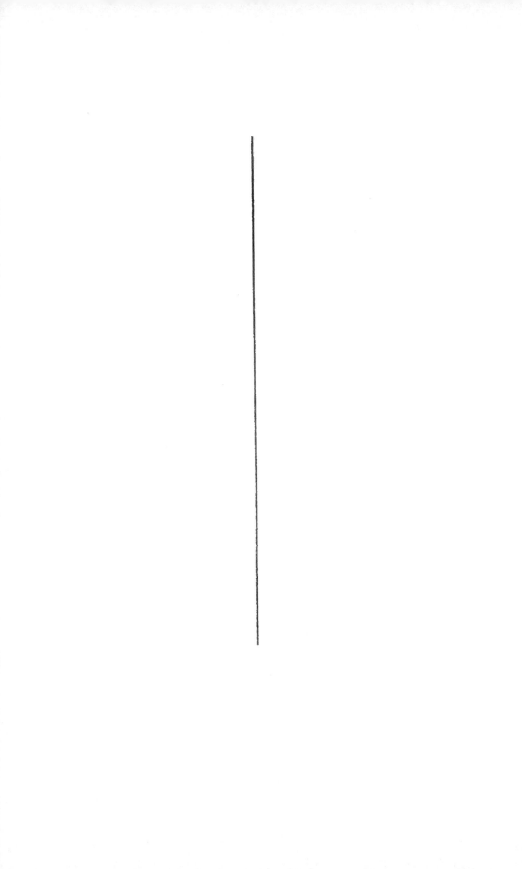

Ingram Content Group UK Ltd.
Milton Keynes UK
UKHW022304260623
424090UK00005B/167

9 781016 723886